THE PATHS
THAT LIE
AHEAD

———∞∘◦❂◦∘∞———

THE PATHS THAT LIE AHEAD

PART ONE: MONEY, POWER, AND BETRAYAL

WRITTEN BY: MELVIN T. LUSTER JR.

Order this book online at www.trafford.com
or email orders@trafford.com

Most Trafford titles are also available at major online book retailers.

Printed in the United States of America.

ISBN: 978-1-4269-7950-7 (sc)
ISBN: 978-1-4269-7951-4 (e)

Library of Congress Control Number: 2011913942

Trafford rev. 08/17/2011

 www.trafford.com

North America & international
toll-free: 1 888 232 4444 (USA & Canada)
phone: 250 383 6864 ♦ fax: 812 355 4082

INTRODUCTION

A bunch of angry high school students are gathering in the high school cafeteria. As the students gather they seem to be very hostile and threatening to one another. Racial slurs are being shouted back and forth. Teachers come and get in the middle of the hostile gathering of students. The crowd is now divided; blacks on one side and whites on the other, and as I look around I realize I'm stuck right smack dab in the middle of this entire ruckus. The angry black and white students start pushing one another and a few fist begin to fly. Next thing I know Ms. Burns the principle comes and grabs me and drags me out of the middle of this hostile crowd by my arm. She is practically pulling me to her office and as we get there she pushes me into one of the chairs in front of her desk. She begins to speak to me but her speech seems to be muffled and isn't making sense. I was already confused about what's going on, but now I'm even more confused. I hear a very big commotion going on behind me; I turn around to see what's going on. It's my mother and she is very upset, but for some reason every word she speaks seems to be muffled just like Ms. Burns's speech, and her words are not making sense either. She smacks me in my head, then grabs me by the collar of my shirt and pulls me to the car. As she drives she's crying and she continues to speak and yell out muffled words at me. But I get the point, somewhere I must've messed up; so I hold my head down in disappointment and start feeling sorry for myself. **All of a sudden!!!** I start hearing loud claps and cheers. The loud claps and cheers kind of startle me a little bit. So I look up and look out of the passenger side window, and to my surprise people where lined up and down the side-walk in front of the coliseum and they seemed to be cheering me on. Dang what a sudden change of events; I begin to think to myself, "What in the world is going on", I'm beyond confused now. I look down at myself and now it appears I'm in a graduation gown. I look over at my mother and I notice that her sadness and tears have been turned *into joy and smiles. As I notice the sudden change that has taken place around me I couldn't help but wonder once again "what's going on".* **BEEP! BEEP! BEEP!** I rise up and hit the snooze button on the alarm clock; that's when I realized that this was just another dream.

CHAPTER 1
GETTING READY FOR SCHOOL

HEADING OUT TO SCHOOL

As I give a big morning stretch and yawn, I sit up on the edge of my bed slowly because I really don't feel like getting up. Wiping the sleep from my eyes I look over at the alarm clock thinking, 630 came way too fast. I wouldn't even be up this early if hadn't of been on the phone most of the night talking to my girl like I'm never going to see her again. But I have to go to school so I might as well get over it. I go to the bathroom and turn on the shower; I get me a towel and a wash cloth and hang them up on the shower pole. Before I get in the shower I take a long morning pee, and I know yaw know how that first of the morning pee feels, *"AH!!!"* I get in the shower and let the warm water hit my back first; I grab my wash cloth and start washing myself. After I wash my hair I reach for my towel with my eyes closed because I hate having water on my face, but my towel is gone. Messy Marvin must be in here, that's what I call my younger brother Lee; He's in the ninth grade and he act just like it.

With a little frustration in my voice I say, "Man, give me my towel please".

"What towel?"

"Come on Lee quit playing"!

1

Forget it, so I start wiping the water off my face with my hands like I see swimmers do when they get out of the pool. I step out of the shower with my eyes partly open; I see my towel on the toilet seat and grab it. I vigorously start drying myself off staring at Lee the whole time like I'm going to kill him.

"You play way too much!"

I wrap my towel around my waist and then shove him out from in front of the mirror while he was brushing his teeth and start brushing mine. He didn't like it but what's he going to do I'm big brother. While I was brushing I notice he had a mouth full of tooth paste to spit out, so I hurried up and finished and moved out the way so he could finish. I nudged him again on my way out of the bathroom and headed to my bedroom to get dress for school.

"I can't stand you!"

See, Lee don't mind aggravating you, but if you aggravate him, he'll get mad and all bent out of shape like you trying to kill him.

"Yaw better stop making all that damn noise and get ready for school", my moms shout from her bedroom!

But you have to know my brother, for some reason he always has to try to have the last word so he responds in a softer calmer voice, "But he started it".

"I don't care who started it, I'm stopping it", and the argument ended on that note.

After we get dressed we go into our mama's room so we can give her a kiss and say see you later before we leave out for school.

"Mama we about to leave"!

She turns with a smile on her face and her mornings breathe humming and says, "O.K I love yaw, don't forget to lock the door, and Milton I want you to know that I'm very proud of you."

2

I look back and crack a smile; Lee runs in behind me in a hurry and gives her a kiss, and then we both run down the stairs. I lock the door like mama said, we lined up like racers in front of the outside steps, and race to the bus stop; which you know I won.

~~~ ~~~ ~~~

MEETING UP WITH VIKKI

As the bus pulls up to the school to let us off; we all file off and head to the cafeteria because that's the designated area were we can hang out, of course eat breakfast, and wait for the homeroom bell to ring. As we come through the cafeteria doors Lee starts being Lee meaning immature.

Seeing Vikki he says to me, "There's your sweetie pie."

I put him in a headlock and respond, "Don't start heady Murphy."

I let him go and then I gave Vikki a hug, "What's up baby."

"Nothing much just waiting on you"

Lee snickers, Vikki blushes a little and then says to him, "I see you being your usual self today?"

Everyone knows how messy Lee is. She turns and looks at me with her beautiful brown eyes as the line moves a little forward and says, "Next Friday we graduate."

"I know can you believe it?"

"Milton I'm so proud of you. You worked really hard over the past two years. You have a 3.0 grade point average, and you going to college", when she said college she got sad.

"Baby please come on; let's not talk about that right now?"

"Why do you want to go to school way in Alaska when you can go to a good school right here in Tennessee with me?"

"Sweetie I told you I just want to get away from here. I feel like if I stay here I'm bound to get in some kind of trouble."

"If you leave me how will we ever be together?"

We reach the cashier and as she gets ready to pay for her food I stop her and tell her, "You know I got you", I would've paid for Lee's but he ran off with his friends.

"Baby I might not even get accepted."

"With a GPA like yours and SAT scores as high as yours. Trust me you getting in."

"Well let's not worry about that right now, since we already graduating is their anything wrong with us concentrating on one another for awhile?"

"I love you."

"I love you to."

So we eat, laughing and joking with one another; making fun of Lee and his friends, and how stupid they be acting. The bell rings and everyone gets up and start filing out the cafeteria headed to their homeroom.

"All right big bro"!

"All right little homie"!

Vikki and I have the same homeroom so we walk to class together like always holding hands. We sit down at our desk the bell rings again and a few more people come running in like they aren't already late, but who cares we're seniors and this is our last full week.

"You know I'm really going to miss you."

"Vikki come on now I haven't even been accepted yet."

Then all of a sudden the intercom comes on with the morning school news. After giving all the school news the secretary then says, *"Milton Lusser, please come to the office, Milton Lusser please come to the office!"*

"I wonder what this is all about."

~~~ ~~~ ~~~

TALKING TO THE COUNSELOR

I walk into the school office and the school secretary is on the phone; so I call myself waiting patiently, but I think she thought I was trying to rush her. She puts the phone on her shoulder with a little attitude and says, "Yes may I help you?"

"Yes ma'am, you called for me to come to the office I'm Milton".

She looks on her desk moving a few papers around, I guess she found what she was looking for because then she says, "Milton your guidance counselor Ms. Smart wants to see you in her office."

"Thank you".

I headed to her office hoping everything is o.k. I'm pretty sure it is because this woman has stuck her neck out for me. If it wasn't for her I wouldn't be graduating next week. See this is what happened: About two and a half years ago a white student named Dawn Chambers called me a *"nigger"* in front of everyone in class, the reason why is irrelevant. So you know what I did? I smacked the hell out of her. Was I wrong? Of course I was. What happen next was very surprising. All the white students jumped up on her side, and the blacks on mine. Being honest you could always feel the racial tension that was in the air, it's been there since the school year started. I mean, they brought a bunch of black project kids together with a bunch of rich uppity white kids. So needless to say I got expelled from school why she was only suspended for two days, and I missed a whole year of schooling; because back then there weren't any alternative schools. Ms. Smart thought that the punishment for me was very unfair and unjust. So she fought and fought until she got me back in school. Then she signed me up with correspondence courses that helped me get caught back up to where I needed to be with my credits. It wasn't easy and it took a lot of hard work and dedication; but I made it, thanks to Ms. Smart.

I knock on her office door and she shouts, "Come in!"

"How you doing Ms. Smart I hope everything is alright?"

"Oh yes, everything is just fine, I just wanted to give you this letter from the College of Alaska that came in the mail this morning."

I'm a little shocked by her statement because I was waiting for this letter to come to my home, and was wondering why it was taking so long. I forgot I put the school address as for my return address. I nervously take the letter from Ms. Smart hand and sits down. As I slowly open the blue thick envelop, and pull the letter out. I speed read the entire letter down to where it says, **"YOU HAVE BEEN ACCEPTED AND GIVEN A FULL ACADEMIC SCHOLARSHIP."**

I jump up shouting, "Wooooooo!" pumping my fist in the air.

"Milton calm down, calm down; allow me to be the first to congratulate you." With a big smile on her face I could tell that she was just as excited as I was.

"Thank you Ms. Smart."

"No thank yourself, because you did this."

CHAPTER 2
GRADUATION DAY IS COMING

EMOTIONAL MOMENT

As we get off the school bus and start heading home Lee takes off running like he always does, and I'm walking with a good friend of mine from the neighborhood whose name is Desmond. As we approach the housing project where we live, we see a couple of our childhood friends posting on the corner doing what they dropped out of school to do. For the past three years all they did was sell drugs, and their names where Robert and DJ.

So I shout out, "What's up Rob, what's up DJ!"

"What's up Millie Mil and Des, I see you two made it, congratulation homies", Robert shouts!

DJ must've been really high because his reaction time was slow as hell; well then again he's always been kind of slow motion. With his red eye's he throws up deuces and says, "What's up Milton and Des, congratulation on graduating, I wish I could've made it, but this money was calling my name", and then him and Robert gives one another some dap.

See I've always been attracted to the drug lifestyle for some reason. I've always wanted to be a hustler, a money-maker, and a go getter; why, I don't know. Was it the money, yeah it could've been; maybe it was the women, shit that's a definite "HELL YEA!" or it was probably the cars that they drove. Hell, like I said I don't know, but the truth of the matter was Ms. Princess D. Lusser isn't going; that's my mama's real name.

"What yaw been doing all day".

"Shit what kind of question is that; you already know."

Then Robert pulls out a fat bank roll of money and says to me, "Milton you already know we money makers."

Out of nowhere Desmond says, "Man I better get home before my mama comes outside tripping."

Robert and DJ kind of snicker; then DJ says to me, "shouldn't you be getting home too before your mama come up here tripping on you again?"

"Don't play me like that homie, I'm grown now." But they were right, the last time I hung out up here on this corner trying to sell drugs someone went and told my mama and she came up here and got me. She embarrassed me pretty good to.

"Yeah, I better get home", and they busted out laughing, I gave both of them some dap then I dipped out. Just as I reached the steps in front of our apartment Lee came out the door on his way to get me.

"Mama told me to come get you".

"I'm here now so you can go on back in the house."

As we both go in I start running up the stairs, just when I got half way up, my mama shouts, "Milton come here please!"

"Yes ma'am?"

She was sitting at the table drinking grape juice or at least that's what it looked like and she says to me, "Have a sit I want to talk to you", so I have a seat across from her.

"Son you know how much your mama loves you; I mean, just think back to all the stuff we been through. I called you in here to tell you how proud I am of you. Baby boy you beat the odds that were stacked against you, and next Friday my baby is graduating. I just wanted to have a little heart to heart with you about life son. I know I can't teach you how to be a man only a man can do that, but I can warn you about what you will face in life and how you can deal with it."

So I give her my undivided attention because I wanted to hear what she has to say; she places her hand on my hand and says, "Son life is full of choices, and there will be many different paths that will come in a person's life that one must make a choice about, and that includes you. Some people will make good decisions while others will make bad ones. I want you to know that there are always consequences with every decision that you make good or bad. Son, whatever you do, I want you to choose the right path for your life, whatever it is you decide to do in life make good decisions?"

When she finished talking to me, I thought to myself now is the best time to tell her about my acceptance letter from the College of Alaska.

"Mama I have some good news for you."

"What news is better then your graduation"?

I go into my school bag and pull out the thick blue envelop, I hand it to her and at the same time I say, "I got accepted into college!"

She snatches the letter from my hand and reads it; she screams and starts praising God with tears running down her face shouting, "Thank you Jesus, thank you Jesus, my baby is going to college, thank you Lord!"

Lee comes running in looking like something's wrong asking, "What's going on?"

"Your brother got accepted into college!"

With excitement in his voice he says, "What college are you going to big bro?"

"The College of Alaska"

His excitement disappeared and his smile turned into a frown, and he runs off and goes to his room slamming the door behind him, and I stand there shocked and surprised by his reaction.

"Don't pay him any attention Milton you know he loves and looks up to you, you're his best friend and now you leaving him, he's really going to miss you, but he'll be ok."

As my eyes fill with tears I think to myself "I'm really going to miss him too".

MEETING MY DAD FOR THE FIRST TIME

The following week the seniors didn't have to go to school, that meant for most of the day I didn't have to be bothered with my messy little brother. It was about 10:30 in the morning I was just lying in the bed looking up at the ceiling thinking about how much the Lord has blessed me and my family. All morning long I could hear my mama down stairs talking to someone on the phone. About an hour after she had got off the phone there was a knock at the door. My mama answers and there was a short pause, I could hear whispering but I couldn't understand what was being said; then she screams up the stairs, "Milton come down here I want you to meet someone?"

I'm thinking to myself who in the world is she trying to introduce me to? So I jump up out the bed, threw on a shirt and some shorts, and slowly walk down stairs. I'm really not in a hurry to find out what's she trying to do and wish I could act like I didn't hear her calling me, but that's impossible as loud as she is. When I get down stairs there's this man sitting on the couch and what looks like seventy's style clothing. He had a goal tee and his hair was like a mini afro with a cow lick. So I look over at my mama and defensively point at him and say, "Who is this?"

"This is your father."

"My father"!

"Yes your father and I told him you were graduating Friday and that you wanted him to be there".

I stand there thinking to myself, eighteen years has gone by and I had never seen or heard from this man. This low down, low life dirty sorry excuse for a man, and now he pops up in my life and my mama wants me to act like everything is o.k.

"Milton for what it's worth I want to apologize for not being there for you and your brother when yaw needed me the most."

"How could you go all this time and not contact us or not even want to see us?"

"Son I regret everyday the time I missed with you and your brother, Milton all I'm asking for now is a chance to be your dad?"

For some reason in my heart I believed him, hell we look just alike. We stared at one another for a moment and then he gave me a hug and to be honest I hugged him back.

"Can I take you out to lunch?"

"Sure."

So I ran up the stairs and got dressed. The time I spent with my dad that day really wasn't that bad. The conversations we had got so good, that we lost track of time. I had a good time listening to him talk about the good old days. He talked about how he and mama met, he told me about the good times they shared, he talked about her mama and his mama, he talked about why they broke up, and he even talked about and tried to justify why he didn't come around when we were growing up. Honestly, it was a sorry excuse, but I didn't care, all I ever wanted was my daddy. By the time he took me home Lee was there and his response to our dad showing up in our life unexpectedly was the complete opposite of mine.

EMOTIONAL GOOD-BYE

Being up on that stage made me feel so proud of myself; watching my family and friends cheering me on sent chills up my body. When Ms. Burns finally called my name it seemed as if my whole family went crazy and erupted in cheers. As I looked out into the crowd I seen my mama crying and she blew me a kiss, Lee was standing up going from side to side pointing at me saying, "That's my big brother right there!"

I notice my dad sitting next to my mama and he had on a blue plaid looking suit. I mean, this suit was so seventies, so crazy looking, and ugly; but I could tell that he was just glowing with pride, and he was just clapping away. For some reason I couldn't get the big ass grin he had on his face out my mind, and then I thought to myself, "Damn, I look just like him".

We all gathered in front of the coliseum and took our caps off and threw them in the air; making it official high school was over.

Later on my mama threw a little get together; all my family, friends, and even some church members came by. I could see and hear how proud she was as she talked to our guest. Vikki also stopped by and we sat on the front porch talking because we both knew in a couple of months we would be going our separate ways.

"Well we did it", I replied as I grab her hand.

"Yeah we did".

"Vikki all through high school it's been me and you."

"Every since ninth grade"

"Do you remember how we met?"

"How can I forget"?

Letting go of her hand and placing my arm around her and squeezing her tight like I never want to let her go I said, "We were in gym and I was shooting hoops with the fellas and one of my shots didn't even come close to the rim and the ball hit you right on the head."

"Yeah, and it hurt to."

"It looked like it did".

"Every since then we've been together; Milton I love you and I'm so glad you came into my life."

"I am too."

We kissed like we never kissed before, then she took my hand and placed it between her legs, and I took hers and placed it on the hard bulge in my pants. We stopped kissing and stared in one another eyes for a moment, then she said softly in my ear, "Let's sneak up stairs to your room?" and we did.

We both were virgins up until this point, but eight minutes later that all came to and end. We lost our virginity to one another and spent the next couple of months together; it was a very special time for both of us as we made love three more times since the first time.

Then came time for me to leave and Vikki rode with us to the airport; we held one another not wanting to let go, tears ran down both of our faces. We kissed and the last words we said to one another were, "I love you."

I hugged and kissed my mama, I hugged my brother, and I hugged my dad. I could see them watching as the plane was getting ready to take off. My mama and Vikki cried the whole time; Lee was trying to be strong, but I know he cried when he got home.

CHAPTER 3
ALASKA HERE I COME

WELCOME TO THE COLLEGE OF ALSAKA

T his was my first time flying and I was scared as hell. I just knew we were going to crash. After the plane took off the first ten minutes I was a nervous wreck; the stewardess gave me some kind of pill, and after that I calmed down, relaxed, and then I fell asleep. Each time we took off from an airport a stewardess would give me the same pill; the only time I woke up was when the plane landed. First we landed in Salt Lake City, Utah, now that was a big airport, I didn't think I would ever make it to my next gate; I seen the Rocky Mountains up close and they were huge. Next we landed in Tacoma, Washington right outside of Seattle and it was there that I met up with other students headed to the same college I was headed to. I was very impressed with the diversity of students that the College of Alaska admitted; there were a total of 25 and we came from all over. There were students coming from Mississippi, North Carolina, Florida, Texas, I was the only one from Tennessee, but most were from California. We made one more stop in Anchorage, Alaska and then we finally landed at our *"final destination"*, as the pilot said over the intercom. After I got my luggage I followed the instructions gave to me in my acceptance letter. This airport was very small compared to the ones we just came from; it didn't take long for me to spot the tan colored van parked out front with the College of Alaska written on the side of it in blue letters. So I went outside heading towards the van and as I walked I started looking around at the scenery and it was definitely a culture shock to me. Coming from Knoxville, Tennessee to Fairbanks, Alaska was going to be a big change, and another thing I was wondering about was; "where is the snow"? Then this nerdy looking white guy with brown glasses, a blue and white striped shirt, sandals, and khaki shorts got out the van holding a sign saying, "C.O.A students right here", so we all met up were he was.

"Welcome to the College of Alaska. I'm your transportation to school and my name is Peter Hayes. When we get to the school there will be someone calling out names, if your name is called you are to go with that person because they have been assigned to assist you in getting your schedules, showing you around the campus, and finding your dorm room. So if this is everyone let's load up and head out."

So we all started loading up on the van, me being the gentleman that I am, let the ladies get on first. After we all got in the van we headed to the campus. On the drive to the school I leaned back in my seat and took in the scenery. When we pulled up at the school I was very impressed with its size, and how nice the school looked. When we all got off the van there were some people shouting out names just like Peter said. Then all of a sudden this tall black guy who looked like he could be a basketball player called mine, "Milton Lusser!"

"I'm right here."

After he called out about two more names and seen that we were all present he then introduced himself, "My name is Marquez Whiteside and I've been assigned to be your campus guide."

He took us to registration and then to the financial aide office, we got our schedules, our dorm room keys and then he took us to our dorms where he turned us over to our dorm leader. My dorm leader introduced himself as David Walker. He was a heavy set man who I thought was going to die as he showed us to our rooms, he was breathing real hard and every now and then he had to stop and catch his breathe. But he was well dressed and you could tell that he really cared about his appearance.

As he showed us to our rooms he reminded us, "Don't forget tomorrow you will have to go down to the personnel office and get your student ID's made."

I was the last one he showed their dorm room to and just like the four people before me he said to me, "Here you go, if you have any questions or complaints I'm on the first floor in room 101." Then he walked off.

As I went into my dorm room I was very excited, but I kept it all on the inside. I looked around at the room and then it sunk in; this was going to be a fresh start for me. I hated my name "Milton" so I decided right then to switch my first and middle name. My middle name was Andre and it just sounded much more cooler and lady like. I realized that these people don't know anything about me; so that meant I could portray myself to be whoever I wanted to be, and they wouldn't even know. So right then I decided to be a go getter and right after thinking that the door open and I jumped because it startled me.

"Oh my bad, I didn't mean to scare you".

"Naw you straight I was just thinking; Andre", sticking out my hand.

He shakes it and says, "Permious." Wow what a name I thought to myself; Permious was 6'3, around 200 pounds, he was very solid looking and intimidating, and he always kept a shaved head.

"What side of the room you want?"

"It don't matter to me, you was here first".

So to end the back and forth before it really got started I grabbed my stuff and took it to the left side of the room. We both started to unpack and at the same time we talked trying to get to know one another or better yet; sizing one another up.

"Where you from homie"?

"Knoxville, Tennessee; and you"

"Greensboro, North Carolina"

"How did you hear about the wonderful and great College of Alaska"?

"On the student board at my school, I was looking for a school away from home, and I saw this one; It didn't look too bad so I was like, why not; what about you"?

"Pretty much the same, my school counselor helped me locate a good school away from home".

"Do you have any brothers and sisters"?

"Yeah, I have a younger brother and you"?

"I'm an only child, do you play any sports".

"Man I'm one hell of a basketball player".

"I hear you, but I don't think you can handle me though".

"Oh yeah, don't let the size fool you".

"We're going to have to hit the court one day".

"No doubt"

"We also need to find us some pussy", and I just cracked a smile.

The one thing that I noticed about Permious as we continue to talk was that he was definitely a player. Well, at least that's how he seemed. When we finished unpacking our stuff we both were hungry, so we found our way to the cafeteria and through down on a couple of cheeseburgers and fries. Everything so far seems to be starting off pretty good, but for some reason I'm just so determined to depict myself as a real bad ass. I'm just wondering; how far will faking it really get me?

GOING TO CLASS

Starting off everything was good, and if you have time allow me to explain why I say this. I was a business major and I took my personal goals real serious. I was in class on time everyday, I hit the books hard, and I stayed on top of everything my professors where teaching me. While my roommate rarely ever came home; if I wasn't at home studying I was at the library. See I wasn't focused on partying and on girls like everyone else was, my attention was completely on my books and I went to every available study hall pertaining to my classes that I could. I had four classes a week, two were in the morning, and the other two were in the afternoon. The results of me focusing completely on my classes was that I passed every mid-term and final exam with perfect scores, and my grade point average was a 4.0, and I was very proud of myself. Even though I couldn't afford to go home like everyone else could on holidays; I would just send my mama copies of my grades. Whenever I would talk to her on the phone and back then cell phones didn't exist you had to call home collect, I could tell she was proud of me.

One night to my surprise Permious came home, and whenever he did he was only here for three reasons: to shower, change clothes, and pick with me. See I never quite understood why he would be gone for days at a time and then come home with the same clothes on and clean his self up, think about that?

"Dre it's more to the college life then just studying".

"I know, but I didn't come here to do what you're doing, I came to get a degree."

"Hell me to, but I also came to have fun to!"

"I know you did homie don't take what I'm saying the wrong way, but I'm focused on my studies and you should be to, their will be plenty of time for parties and girls."

"While you sitting up here studying all day tell me what fun have you had since you been here?"

"Look that's just how I see it."

"No Dre tell me what fun have you had since you been here"?

So I start thinking to myself and I mean for a good five minutes and I couldn't come up with anything, then he says, "In college you are suppose to create memories, that's what I'm doing and that's what you should be doing too. When your kids ask you about your college years your stories are going to be boring."

Now he has me thinking because I don't want to be boring, but at the same time I don't want to lose focus of what I'm here for.

"You told me that you're always the life of the party back home."

"I am"!

"I can't tell, all I ever see you doing is studying, eating, and sleeping."

By this time Permious was fully dressed and as he sits on his bed to put on his shoes he says, "Dre there's nothing wrong with what you're doing I'm just giving you a hard time, as a friend I just want you to lighten up a little bit and have some fun."

"What you wanting me to do homie?"

"Don't go any where, stay right here I got a surprise for you", then he jumps up and runs out the room.

As you can see I'm easily influenced. I grab my head phones and turned on some Tupac's "Me against the World", lay down, and then I dosed off. I don't know how long it was before Permious came back, but when he came back he had two of the finest black girls on campus with him.

He touched me on my shoulder and wakes me up and says, "This is my home girl Keshia and her friend Kayla and she wants to have a good time if you catch my drift", and then he winks at me.

He didn't have to wink because I understood perfectly well what he was saying. So I sit up on the edge of my bed and she says, "Damn, you fine as hell."

"Thank you, you fine as hell too."

"My girl is spending the night with Permious; do you mind if I spend the night with you?"

"Sure!" She could tell I was nervous as hell, but for some reason she was still very persistent and determine, like she really wanted me; why I have no idea.

Permious places a box of condoms on the dresser between our beds and turns off the lights. I can faintly see because the light from outside the window was glowing in and I could tell that she was getting undressed. Looking in her direction I notice that her body was banging and that she was so damn sexy. She gets under the covers with me smelling so damn good; like a field of French Vanilla flowers. We start caressing, licking, and kissing on one another's hot spots for a while, getting one another all hot and horny. I could slightly taste and smell the alcohol on her breath, but I didn't care. We softly and slowly start kissing, and the rest is history. First, I start kissing on her neck, I move to her breast where I sucked, licked, and kissed on them for a while, next I move down between her legs where I kissed on each part of her leg up close near her pussy, and finally I started eating her pussy and sucking on her clique; and I didn't miss a beat. The next thing I know she explodes in my mouth multiple times.

Then she says, "Damn baby I want you to put it in", so I stop licking on her pussy, wipe my mouth, grab a condom, and give her what she wanted.

I'm going to work on one side of the room and Permious on the other. It didn't happen over night but this was the start of my down fall. I slowly began to lose my focus because I started feeling like I was the man, "Hell!", after tonight I know that I'm the man.

MAKING FRIENDS

After what happened the other night I kind of loosened up a little bit. I started chilling and hanging out with Permious more; I started going clubbing and watching movies in the dayroom with him and other dorm residents. Kayla gave a brother the big head because she kept coming back. She didn't want a relationship and neither did I. All she wanted was sex and the sex was off the chain. One night while we were all in the dayroom watching the movie "Friday" with Ice Cube and Chris Tucker, do you remember the part when Smokey called Big Worm-Big Perm? Right after Smokey said that I looked over at Permious and said, "What's up Big Perm!"

Everyone in the dayroom busted out laughing, but Permious got real upset and acted like he wanted to fight me because everyone was laughing at him.

"Permious calm down; I was just joking with you."

He got up and stormed out the dayroom. Permious hated that name at first, but over time it kind of grew on him, and then that was all he was known by; either we called him "Big Perm" or we would just called him "Perm". Perm and I would also reenact the Craig and Smokey porch scene, and people use to love it. Every time people seen us they wanted us to do Craig and Smokey and we would.

I even met some cool ass black people who were born and raised in Alaska, and yes there are black folks in Alaska. See there's a couple of military bases up there and that's how most of the blacks up there got there. These families liked Alaska so much that they decided to stay, can you believe that? Plus you get a dividend check once a year if you're a resident, and that's each person in the house.

Allow me to introduce the crew that I ran with to yaw: There was Marcus Tipson who had finger waves in his head (That's a West Coast thang), He was around 5'6, 230lbs, and his family was originally from Sacramento, California. This brother loved making, writing, and listening to music; there was Kelvin Tate who had braids in his head before braids were popular. He was around 5'4, 120lbs; we also called him "Money Kell"; he was from Alaska and actually did time in prison up there for selling dope; there was Javonte' Jones and he tried so hard to be like Money Kell, but his hair always stayed nappy as hell the complete opposite of Money Kell his role model. He was about 5'8, 155lbs; he was also from Alaska and he was Money Kell's little cousin. He was really too young to be hanging with us but we let him; and last of all there was Manly and he didn't have much of a style at all. He had a mini fro, but he kept it combed. He was about 6'0, 250 plus; he was from Atlanta and had a mouth full of gold, truthfully this brother was a real ass thug, but he was also down and cools as hell. We called our selves the "Too Real Click", and it was with these brothers that I hit my first blunt. I had never smoked anything before, but you know me I'll fake it until I make it. One night we were all over at Javonte's house which was the hang out, just chilling. We were drinking Hennessy and they were smoking that skunk smelling weed; usually I would let the blunt pass me by or I would grab it and pass it on. But on this particular night I grabbed it, held it for a moment, and then I hit it.

I choked like I never had before; Perm looks over at me and says with concern in his voice, "Dre what are you doing, you don't smoke!"

"Damn homie you O.K", Javonte asked?

I'm choking but I'm trying to talk at the same time, but I can't get it out, then Money Kell says, "Dre that's some good ass weed we be blowing on, we call that Alaska's finest and if you don't know what you doing it can put a real hurting on you."

Money Kell gets up and goes and gets me some water, it kind of calmed the choking down but my chest was still on fire.

"Dre you alright"

If you are reading this book, and if you don't mind, allow me to explain my first experience with smoking weed? I could hear my heart beating and I mean it was pounding and it sounded and felt like it was trying to get out my chest, people from somewhere was talking, at the time I didn't know from where I just thought I was hearing voices, but later I realized that it was the T.V. My body was tingling so bad that I thought I was going to die. I really thought, and it really felt like my spirit was trying to leave my body. I might not have known what I was doing but I must've done something right because I don't remember how I got to my dorm room the next day.

The next day when I woke up I couldn't remember anything. So I just lay in the bed for a few more minutes or at least that's how long it seemed. I got up and dragged myself to the cafeteria thinking that it was still breakfast time, but when I got there that's when I found out that it was 6'oclock in the evening. See in the fall and winter times the sun rarely ever comes up in Alaska and it's so easy to get your times confused. So I got me a sandwich and a bag of chips, and then I went back to my dorm room.

When I got back Perm was there and he was like, "Damn homie you were messed up last night."

"I must've been because I can't remember anything".

"I know you don't, we had to drag and sneak your butt up past Walker who was out larking, looking for a reason to write someone up."

"What yaw doing tonight?"

"Shit, the same ole, same ole".

After I ate my sandwich and chips, I washed my face and brushed my teeth, and then I headed out with Perm to his Toyota Celica. We went to the same spot, we went to every night; Javonte's house, and this time when we got there Money Kell had some fine ass girls there dancing and stripping like we at a strip club; that's just how he was a true party animal. I go to the kitchen were the so called major players were and once again the blunt was going around the table. I let it pass me up the first time, but it was very tempting; then out of the blue Money Kell turns up the stereo blasting Master P and starts free styling and his flow was tight as hell. Then Big Manly jumps in and his flow was off the chain to. Everyone except me was giving it a try including the strippers.

Then Perm looks over at me with his red low eyes and says, "Come on Dre get some of this!"

"Naw I'm good."

Deuce tries to hand me the blunt and I was like, "Naw I'm straight."

"Dre hit the blunt, it will help get your mind right".

The weed smelled so damn sweet and delicious that I couldn't fight the temptation any longer, so I hit it, but not as hard as I did yesterday; and as I was getting ready to choke Deuce says, "Hold it in don't let it choke you."

So I'm struggling to hold it in and all of sudden my body gives three hiccup like reflexes and then stop. Then Deuce said, "Blow it out", and I did. Since this time I never choked again, but I'm really feeling good right now, so I hit the blunt a couple more times then pass it to Manly.

Moving his head to the beat of the music Deuce looks over at me and says, "Dre feel the beat."

So I start moving my head to the beat and now I'm feeling it, and then Deuce said something I will never forget, he said, "Now let how you feel come out."

See I've never really been through anything, so what I did was I flowed about the stuff I always wanted to do as if I had. I waited a few minutes still moving my head to the beat and when I let loose, I let loose, I ripped it. I didn't even know I could free style like that everyone was shocked, but not more then I was. For my first time ever doing something like that it was pretty impressive. I never took our free styling serious I just looked at it like it was something we did for fun when we all got together. But whenever you heard Perm talk about it, and when you looked in his eyes you tell he had other things in mind, and I mean big plans.

CHAPTER 4
LOOKING OUT

COME CHECK THIS OUT

The snow is finally gone and the sun is starting to come up! For the last nine months we had to deal with the snow, the extreme cold, and basically no sun. But now Alaska is looking like a totally different place. Now the sun doesn't go down, matter of fact on June 21 they have a celebration because that's the longest day of the year. 2'oclock in the morning looks just like it does at 2'oclock in the afternoon. Some students were going back home for the summer; while others decided to stay and find jobs like myself. The main reason I decided to stay was because I didn't have the money to go home and then get back. So I made plans to stay with Big Perm and one of his girlfriends whose name is Denise. One day Perm and I rode to the weed spot to buy some weed, but when we got there we were told that they were all out, and that was shocking. Then we went to the other side of town to holla at the homeboy over there and he was out to, and that was another surprise. So we sat in the car for a moment thinking who we can get a sack of weed from.

"Let's holla at Money Kell you know he has the connections."

So we rode over to his spot and he had nothing, damn!

"A Big Perm you have time to run me to Burger World so I can get something to eat", Money Kell asks?

"Are you going to get me something?"

"I got you."

I get up and let Money Kell sit in the front seat; not because I had to, I just like riding in the back. When we arrived at Burger World the drive thru line was out the parking lot. So Perm parks and Money Kell turns and asks me, "What you want Dre?"

"Just a double cheeseburger with everything and some fries"

They both got out the car and went into Burger World. I just sat there frustrated because I needed some weed, and then I looked up and saw David Walker the dorm leader coming out the restaurant, so I shout, "What's up David?"

"Oh, what's up Andre, what you been up to?"

"Nothing much, I just can't wait for school to start back." Then we give one another some dap.

"Me to, you know this is my last Semester I graduate in December."

"I didn't know that".

But as we talked I noticed that his eyes looked a little on the low side; so now I'm thinking either he's "sleepy or he smokes weed". I mean, his eyes weren't blood shot red, but he could've used Visine. This is sad, but that's how damn bad I'm craving some weed, so after debating it momentarily in my head, I finally built up enough nerve to ask him. Now yaw must also understand that this is my dorm leader that I'm getting ready to ask where the weed at.

"A David you know where I can find some green?"

I think my question kind of caught him of guard because he paused and looked around and then said, "What you mean, weed"?

"Yea"

"You don't even know me, so why would you come at me like that"?

"A look I don't mean no disrespect or anything, I don't want to get kicked out of school", but as I'm talking he interrupts me, "Come to the dorm and talk to me, but when you come; come by your self."

I nodded my head "Yes" and then he walked off.

At the same time Perm and Money Kell comes out of Burger World with our food. We ride back to Money Kell's spot; we park so we can eat. We chill there for a minute bumping Tupac's "All Eyez on me."

I nudge Perm and say, "I need you to run me somewhere."

"Where"

"I got one more person I want to check with about some weed."

His face lit up because that's right up his alley. Money Kell gets out the car and says, "If they do let me know so I can get some to." I get up in the front seat, we give Money Kell some dap, and then Perm and I rolled out.

"Where we going Dre"

"To the dorm"

"Who has weed on campus"?

I hesitate because I didn't want to tell him, but this is my homie, "I seen David Walker the dorm leader at Burger World and I asked him if he knew were I could get some weed, and he told me to come holla at him at his dorm room, but I have to talk to him by myself he said."

"You sure you should do that Dre, because first of all he's our dorm leader, and secondly he doesn't look like he would know were some weed would be." Perms right and now he has me second guessing myself, but something in my heart was saying do it,

"Just wait for me; and if it's a trap I'm denying it, and it's my word against his."

We pull up at the dorm; I get out the car and goes to David's room door.

I knock on the door, "Come in", he shouts!

I walk in, and then he says, "Have a seat", so I sit down in the chair by his computer, "What you see going on Andre is a drought."

I'm looking confused and say, "What!"

"When you can't find weed on the streets it's known as a drought meaning it's dried up."

O.K. now I'm starting to understand what he's talking about. Then he takes me over to his closet and says, "You ready"?

He opens the door, and when he opened it you wouldn't believe what I seen. It was a grow room; and it had the sweetest and most potent smell of weed that I had ever smelled, I've heard about these before, but this was my first time ever seeing and smelling the aroma of one. It had eight humongous almost full grown plants in it. These plants stood taller then me, so that should give an idea of how tall these plants were because I'm 5'7. He closed the closet door and we go over to his bed and out from under the bed he pulls out a red and yellow suit case, and when he opened it, it had 17 huge storage bags of weed.

"Each of these bags holds a pound a piece." He grabs one and takes a long dragging smell, and then passes it to me to smell. It had the same skunk like smell of the weed that I had smoked some time back, we been looking for some, but we haven't been able to find any since.

I'm just going to be honest with yaw I was breathless, I had never seen this much weed before in my life.

"So, what you looking for", I'm just standing there speechless; then he says, "Look Andre I wouldn't have showed you my entire grow room if I didn't trust you. I've been watching you every since you got up here and you seem to be cool. I want you to leave this between us, even if you don't agree with what I'm about to ask you, can I trust you?"

"You can trust me homie, but let me ask you a question, you sell weed?"

"I sell it, but not like you would think. I only mess with a select few. Now let me ask you a question; why do you think I'm talking to you and showing you all of this?"

I'm lost and puzzled at that question because I really don't know. Then he replies, "To help me."

"To help you"

He fires up a blunt, puffs on it several times and then passes it to me and says, "Yeah to help me, because the streets are dry and that's good for business. I've always wanted to make more money then what I was making, but I didn't know anyone out in the city I would trust enough to do this kind of business with."

He folds his arms and lean back in his desk chair and says, "But I trust you for some reason and plus I know you know people because of how you came at me at Burger World."

"I do."

"Good here you go."

He gives me one of the 17 storage bags, and in it the weed was already divide up and bagged. "Its 40 baggies in there, and each baggy is to be sold at $40 a piece, now you do the math?"

As I'm thinking he says, "That's $1600, I want you to bring me back a $1000, and you keep the $600. I promise you, you do me right I'll always take care of you; do we have a deal?", and then he holds out his hand for me to shake.

"I grab his hand and shake it and reply, "You have a deal, by the way just call me Dre."

I stuff the weed in the front of my pants and walked out the room. When I get to the car I pull out the weed and showed Perm. I tell him everything David said to me and he was shocked; I didn't tell him about the grow room because I believe something's you need to keep to yourself. I took Perm in as a partner, and agreed to split my share with him since we did ride around together making sales, and he made it clear that he had my back no matter what. So what we would do is separate David's share off the top and made his money first. In fact, that night we brought him his money within four hours, that's how dry the streets were. We had the right connections on both sides; Money Kell because he knew people and David because he supplied it. In two days we made over $8000 after we took David his cut; now that was some big business. If you thought we were doing it big then; Shit that was just the beginning. Trust me it's going to get bigger and better so just keep on reading especially if you love seeing the underdog on top.

CAN YOU DO ME A BIG FAVOR

The summer of '95 was the summer of Dre and Big Perm; we smoked; sold and made so much money off our little weed operation we lost count. David didn't have to do anything but keep us supplied; he kept us supplied and we kept his pockets fat. If you knew me before and you seen me now you wouldn't recognize me. I was now wearing nothing but name brand clothes and shoes, I turned into the Nike man, if you seen me you probably would've thought I had a Nike contract. I'm telling you this summer we did it up and we did it big. Registration for school was August 18, and I didn't have any worries when it came to money. I even helped a few of my friends who were struggling to pay for books and classes. We had gained a lot of respect around the city and on campus, I got to the point were I felt like I was untouchable and when you think like that, believe me, that's some dangerous thinking.

I already know next month the snow and extreme cold is coming, and I feel like we better take advantage and enjoy the good weather while we can. Up here in Alaska we don't have four seasons like other places do, we only have two seasons; summer and winter. Its not that I dreaded the cold, it's just that we made so much money in the summer, I'm kind of nervous that the cold will slow down our operation and we might lose money. That's what I was thinking and worried about, but I was clearly wrong because another drought hit and we were the only ones with weed yet again; don't forget I'm new at this kind of stuff.

Two weeks before Thanksgiving I came home from class and I was surprised to see a note on my dorm room door. David left me a message to come see him when I had a chance; I'm wondering to myself "What's this all about?" So I took a shower, put on my doo-rag, a tank top t-shirt, some shorts, and headed to his room in my house shoes.

I knock on the door and he shouts, "Come in!" Like he already knew it was me. I go in and see him and his girlfriend hugged up on the bed watching T.V so I say, "What's up David, how you doing Michelle?"

"Babe let me holla at Dre for a minute?"

"Only for a minute because this is our night", she replies.

When she got up and walked out the room David gets up and moves over to his computer desk chair and says, "Homie I need a big favor from you?"

"You mind if I sit down for this"?

"Oh my bad homie, yeah have a sit, you want a coke or something reach in the fridge and grab you something to drink."

"It doesn't involve hurting or killing anyone does it?"

"Hell naw!"

My question must've been funny because he started laughing and I mean he's really cracking up, him laughing so hard causes me to laugh because you know he's big as hell and he sounds and looks just like Santa Clause right now.

As he composes himself, wiping his eyes he says, "Dre all I wanted to ask you is if you would look out for the plants and stuff because I'm going to California with my girl for Thanksgiving to meet her family."

"My bad for coming at you like that homie, sure I got you."

"Before I leave I'll show you what I need you to do."

"Alright big homie just let me know when and I'll be here."

"Oh yeah while I'm gone any money you make, you keep a $1000 and give me $600."

"Really"!

"Trust me, I said I'll never mess you over."

We gave one another dap again and I leave out.

Two days before he got ready to leave we hooked up and he showed me what I needed to do, and he wanted me to do this all by myself. He was gone for two weeks and while he was gone I sold twelve storage bags of weed. Remember there's $1600 in each bag, and since we reversed the roles on these packages I made $12,000 compared to $7200, and that was gravy. As soon as he got back I gave him his part and then I showed him that I didn't mishandle or mess him over while he was gone, and he was impressed. Big Perm kept saying I was stupid for doing this, but I just knew in my heart that in the long run it was going to pay off, and trust me it will or better yet it did.

CHAPTER 5
OPERATION: IT'S GOING DOWN

I'M GONE YOU CAN HAVE IT

T he biggest playa in Alaska just got married. No I'm not talking about me, I'm talking about Big Perm; Permious Jackson married Denise Weaver and I couldn't believe it, after all I seen this brother do while they were dating.

Perm and his new wife went to there home towns for Christmas break; he's from North Carolina and Denise is from South Carolina. I guess they wanted to be surround by there families and friends, but hell what I'm I? I didn't even know all this went down until he got back; wanting to show me some punk ass wedding pictures.

"Why wasn't I invited again?"

"It was a spare of the moment thing Dre".

"Looking at these pictures it doesn't look like a spare of the moment deal, this wedding looks nice as hell."

"Come on Dre"

After I looked at the pictures I went to the kitchen to where Denise was and said, "Congratulations."

"Thank you Dre", she replies, and I gave her a $100 bill.

I go and get into my new but used car that I just bought; it's a Gold '87 Honda Accord to be exact. Perm comes outside before I pull off and say, "Come on Dre, you right I shouldn't have done it like that."

"Don't worry about it homie, I said it's all good"

We give one another some dap and then I rolled out headed to the campus. I guess I'll be getting a new dorm roommate I think to myself because Perm and Denise have a nice big brick house. Really I'm not mad at Perm, I'm actually very happy for him, I'm just giving him a hard time because I know if I had done him like that he would be upset to. There's another thing bothering me about this situation, Perm has never been faithful to Denise since they have been talking. Maybe he has changed, I doubt it, but there's a first for everything.

I ride around for about thirty minutes bumping Tupac's "Me against the world" album, and then I fire up the half of blunt I had in the ashtray. As I pull up at the dorms I'm shaking my head thinking about ole Permious Jackson, as soon as I get in my dorm room the phone rings; if you haven't noticed by now a car and a phone, shoot a brother done came up.

"Hello?"

"Dre we going to kick it tonight"

"Perm you just got married, spend some time with your new wife".

"Don't worry about that homie, I have that under control, I'm a call the fellas and let them know that it's on."

"Alright it's on".

As soon as I kicked off my shoes and got ready to lie down the phone rings again, "Hello?"

"What's up Dre its David"?

"What's up David everything good?"

"Yeah everything's good; I just need to talk to you when you get a chance".

"I'm on my way".

I get up and through on my house shoes and head to his room, knocking on his door he shouts, "Come on in!"

I go in and to my surprise he has everything just about packed up, looking around I say, "What's up were you going?"

"Dre you know both of us graduated last month, and we decided it's time for us to move back to the lower 48".

"What!"

"Man I'm going back home, my time up here in this ice box is over, it's just gets too damn cold for me to want to stay and raise a family".

I just stand there for a minute shocked, because this bad news has caught me off guard, and then he says, "It's all yours now."

"What you mean its all mine"?

"I broke down the remaining plants I had and bagged them up for you. Plus I already had six storage bags ready to go; this will leave you with fourteen pounds which should hold you over until your next crop comes in."

"Where in the world am I going to put a grow room, the closet in my room is too small; no were near the size of yours."

"Well look, go ahead and take the fourteen pounds now, think about what you want to do about the grow room and let me know by tomorrow".

He gives me a big clothes basket with clothes on top and says, "I'll pick up my clothes tomorrow", we give one another dap then I dipped out.

That night at the night club I wasn't really myself and Perm could tell. I was thinking about what David had told me, because if we don't keep the weed going then our money making quest is over.

"What's up Dre, are you alright?"

"Yeah I'm straight, why you ask"?

"I mean you just turned down the third girl that asked you to dance and that's not like you."

"Look Perm things are about to change".

We both give Manly some dap as he comes to the table and then he turns towards me and says, "Like what?"

"David is leaving."

"What"!

"Yeah he's leaving in about a week, and he offered to give me his grow room but I don't have any were to put it."

"How much weed do we have?"

"Fourteen pounds; which is only enough to last us for a few months".

"Dre get all the information David is going to give you, we have a basement at the house and we'll put it there until we figure out what to do with it."

"You sure Denise will be cool with that?"

"She likes spending the money I make and if she wants to keep living that kind of life style we have to do what we have to do".

The next day I went and talked to David and he told me everything I needed to know about having a successful grow room. He showed me how to sprout seeds in a damp wash cloth. He told me how long it would take a plant to grow, he told me the difference between a male and a female plant; and to get rid of the male as soon as possible, and finally he told me about the least and the most amount of grams we should get off of each plant. Everything he told me I told Perm; and Perm decided to make our operation even bigger then it was with David. Were David had eight plants, we turned ours into thirty-two, the new plan was to make four times the amount of money we had made with David. We basically supplied the whole city and by that I mean just about every weed smoker bought from us, but for some reason none of the other drug dealers did and that's the group that Perm wanted to target.

We used some of the teenage boys that hung around were we stayed to do runs for us, they didn't go to school anyway so we decided to give them a little job. The money we started making was a little scary at first because we were making so much, but I have to be honest with yaw, it was worth it. I went from being the worker bee to feeling like the king; hell yeah I feel like the weed king!

LET'S DO IT

It's almost harvest time and I'm getting very excited! Three and a half months; that's how long David told us it would take for these plants to grow into full maturity. Honestly they are looking pretty damn good right now, and we are tempted to harvest them today, but the truth of the matter is, it's all a process. We want our weed to be just as good if not better then what David was giving us to sell. In three more weeks we'll see how good we've done in our growth process. We still have five pounds left of the weed David gave us before he left, but business has been kind of slow because we are not the only dealers in town. We know the drought is around the corner and when it hits we want to be prepared and ready to meet the streets needs. I'm just going to keep it real with yaw, my problem is that I'm never planning for the future; I only care about the right now. How much are we going to get; how much are we going to make not tomorrow or next week, but today right now and that can be a problem one day. See while I'm thinking like this, my homie Big Perm isn't he's always planning ahead.

One day while I'm at the dorm in my room just chilling Perm surprisingly stops by. There's a knock on the door and I shout, "Who is it!"

"Perm"!

I jump off the bed to unlock and open the door giving him some dap I say, "What's up homie, is everything O.k?"

"Naw everything good, I just wanted to talk to you about something."

"What's up"?

"Dre when this drought hits I think we need to try to take over and supply everyone that we can. I even mean the other dealers."

"Perm I don't think that's a good idea."

"Why not"!

"Because Perm; #1—we don't produce that much that fast and #2—that's going to draw a lot of unnecessary attention we don't need."

"Dre trust me there's a way of doing everything".

The room gets quite because we both are thinking about what one another just said. He pulls out a sack of the skunk smelling weed we been selling, and a Philly Cigar and starts rolling up.

After he finished twisting and turning he says to me, "Come ride with me so we can talk."

I'm already dressed so all I had to do was put on my shoes, and then we dipped out. When we get in the car Perm hands me the blunt so I could fire it up and I waste no time doing it. I puff on it about five times getting it to burn; blowing the sweet, skunk smelling weed in the air, and then I passed it back to him.

After he puffs on it a few times and blows out the smoke, he passes it back to me and says, "Dre look around you; Fairbanks isn't a very big place and it's without a doubt we get a lot of love and respect from these streets. Everyone knows us and they know we keep that fire."

"True, true"

"Do you know how much you are supposed to actually make off a pound of weed up here in Alaska if you sell it right?"

Passing the blunt back to him I say, "What you mean?"

"David had us selling it all wrong. If we sold a pound the right way we could easily make $3800."

"Yeah right"

"Trust me"

Passing the blunt back to me I say, "How you know that?"

"I did my research".

"Dre if you can sell a pound of weed gram for gram and make $3800, then we should sell our pounds to others dealers for $2500 and plus sell to our regular customers gram for gram."

Passing the blunt back to him I say, "That means our prices are going to have to go up and I don't think our regular customers will go for that."

"Either that or we can make our sacks smaller."

"Perm I don't think anyone will go for that".

Blowing out smoke barely keeping himself from choking, he says, "Hell yea they will!"

"How you know that?"

"First of all, we got that fire; secondly, it's a drought Dre, true smokers will pay whatever they have to in order to get high."

"I don't know Perm".

"We got the man who can help us get this party popping."

"If you think we can make more money then what we were making before; then let's do it."

He hits the little blunt one more time, tosses it out the window, and then he says, "Let's do it then."

Three weeks went by and we went to work in the lab. It took us four days to get everything pulled up, chopped up, pressed, and ready to go. Perm even introduced me to a new method called "cloning". Instead of waiting three and a half months for a crop, it only took us two and a half. Because in cloning you cut off a branch of the original plant, dip the cut part in the cloning solution, place it in a jar of water and wait until you see new roots growing on it, and then you re-plant it; if you compare that to starting from a seed then there's no comparison. Just like clock work the streets were starting to dry up, Money Kell knew the plan, and as soon as the streets got severe he put the plan into motion. At first it was tough, but as time went by it started popping.

MAKING MONEY

Like I said when the drought hit we were ready. Money Kell did his part and Perm and I produced on our end, everything came together just like a hand in a glove. We started supplying the whole city including the other dealers and they didn't even know it. We had a nice little set up going, the only people that could buy weight directly from us was the Too Real crew; Deuce, Money Kell, Manly, and Javonte. Everyone else had to come through them, and they never disappointed when it came to that money. On the outside of the operation it looked like they were pushing there on weed because Perm and I were still dealing with our regular customers, but in actuality during this two year time span 97% of the weed on the streets came from us and the money we made was lovely. The police made there attempts on busting up our money making quest, but all of there attempts were in vain and if one of our little homies did get popped we got them out no second thought or hesitation. What we were doing up in Fairbanks spread all the way down 400 miles away to Anchorage; see they had droughts to. So one weekend Money Kell's home boy Donnie came up

THE PATHS THAT LIE AHEAD

from Anchorage wanting to know how he could get in on the weed action up here. Money Kell played dumb on the first day they talked and as soon as he could he came and told Perm and I what was going on. We met up at Denny's to see what the talk was all about.

Perm and I are already there Money Kell comes in and sits down and says, "What's up Perm, Dre?"

We both give him dap and nod our heads and then I say, "We cool, just wanting to know what's going on and what all the talk is about?"

"One of my homies came up from Anchorage and tells me he knows people down there ready to buy".

"Damn how they know what's going on up here?"

"Shoot I don't know".

Then Perm says, "Look people talk, somebody from down there was probably up here and bought a sack, Shoot who knows, they don't know about me and you and that's all that matters to me."

The waitress comes over and takes our orders for our drinks and then Perm says, "When you say buy is there and offer or can we set the price."

"Well I told him what pounds are going for up here, but I didn't tell him I had the connection yet".

The waitress comes and takes our orders and then Money Kell says, "He showed me the money and told me that he wanted to buy five pounds today, and that he knew a few more people in Anchorage who are ready to buy five pounds a whop to."

"Wait a minute, so what you saying, is that this man wants up to traffic some weed down to Anchorage?"

The waitress brings our food and then Money Kell says, "I think so, look I just wanted to let yaw know what's going on and get yaw opinions before I commit to anything."

"How much is he willing to spend?"

"Around 2500 a pound"

"Go ahead and sell those to him for 2500, and you keep the five hundred off each pound. Call us and let us know what's going on with these cats in Anchorage wanting to do business."

I look at Perm like are you serious, but I didn't say anything because I want to see were Perm is trying to take this.

We eat our food and then we all dip out. Money Kell calls Perm about two hours later with details. Then Perm calls me and wants me to meet him at the mall.

"What's up?"

"What's up", giving one another some dap

"Money Kell called me and told me what these cats in Anchorage want to do."

"What they talking bout?"

"There are five brothers down there that are big time weed dealers, and they are willing to pay 2500 a pound and if we decide to do it, we would deal only with the brother up here now".

"I don't think we should do that Perm, it just seems to be too risky."

"Dre we would only make the trip twice a month making 50,000 each trip, which means we'll make 100,000 a month from this deal, we grow our own weed so that makes this all profit. Taking the 500 off of each pound and giving it to the people who ride with us. We can't beat that; it's not like we don't grow that much. I think we should do it".

"I don't know Perm; I think this would be a very big mistake", then I storm out the store highly upset because I can tell Perm already has his mind made up. I'm headed to my car because I don't have time for all this.

"Dre calm down, look if you not down with it then we won't do it."

"Look you're my best friend and you haven't let me down yet, I can see you already have your mind made up. So guess what, you want to do this, then hell let's do it, but when it back fires don't say I didn't tell you so!"

"We going to meet up with Money Kell's home boy Donnie tonight at the club, I'll pick you up around 10."

I nod my head, stick my hand out the window, we give one another some dap, and then I rolled out.

Later that night we all met up at the club, we had a good time, and we worked everything out with these brothers from Anchorage. Originally Perm was suppose to do the moving, but later I decided that I would be better for that job since Perm had a baby on the way, and I didn't want him to jeopardize his family; that's just the kind of friend I am. I would always take Money Kell and Javonte; we rotated our young teenage workers so they all could make a little money on the side. Perm and I didn't trust anybody with our money especially when you are making this much, that's why we decided one of us would always have to ride, and we were willing to die for our money to. We made a quick 100,000 every month. After each trip I would pay those who rode with me there money; this operation here definitely put us were we needed to be. Perm started buying music equipment setting up there third bedroom as a studio where we would go and free style and get blowed out our minds. I just went splurging crazy, going to strip clubs, buying expense clothes and shoes, and riding clean everyday. If I wanted it I got it, and that includes women to. Now that I think about it I'm glad Perm pushed the issue when it came to expanding our operation, but there's a down side to everything. Like the old saying goes "The more money you make, the more problems you have", and trust me you will see what I mean.

CHAPTER 6
LIVING THE GOOD LIFE

SPENDING MONEY LIKE CRAZY

It seemed like the faster the money was coming the faster we spent it. Whatever we saw and liked we bought it; from shoes and clothes to jewelry. Everyone in our click was living like kings and if they had girlfriends they lived like queens. The motto was whenever I bought something whoever was with me at the time got something to that was just the kind of brother I was. The whole click like I said stayed G-ed up; $1000 a piece ear rings, $250 each shirts and jeans, and $200 pairs of tennis shoes. It was no secret that we had money and was shining, it was no doubt we was balling, but we were balling out of control which isn't a good thing. If the women hadn't notice before they were definitely taking notice now. Perm bought him a '97 fully loaded Cadillac and his wife a '98 Lexus. I bought me a '98 Honda Passport fully loaded and I put three 12 inch speakers in the back. So everywhere I drove I left and impression if you know what I mean. I got me a little spot off campus that I fixed up really nice buying nothing but the best. Forget renting anything we were buying with straight out cash, and there were no complaints. The malls in Fairbanks and Anchorage boomed with our business, I would like to think we had something to do with the economic jump that took place in those cities. I have to admit everything was turning out pretty damn good. Being as small as Fairbanks is you would've thought this was impossible to do, but we were doing it. Maybe we could've, no better yet, we should've done better with the money we were making especially me. But for some reason it was burning a hole in our pockets and we got the big heads thinking we couldn't be stopped.

We would hit Perm's studio at least once a week but a lot of our time we just rode around making our presences known; sitting on our 20 inch chromed out wheels and window rattling sound systems you couldn't tell us anything. All we did all day was twist up blunt after blunt I can't remember one time when I wasn't high. Sometimes we would even through weed parties were we would allow certain people to come and get high on us. This was the way Perm and I would experiment and see what the people liked and what they didn't. The rest of our time was spent in the strip and night club. We would V.I.P our section ourselves and by doing this the ladies just flowed to us. Even though Perm was married he still messed around; he even got one of his creep moves a nice spot on the other side of town. As we sat at our table with women all around us Perm leans over and says, "When we first started this is this what you envisioned?"

I hesitated for a moment, looked around, and hit the blunt then I said, "Honestly no, but now that we have it I wouldn't trade for the world."

We bumped fist with one another and both leaned back in our seats and I thought to myself "Damn it feels good to be me".

ME AND MY WOMEN

Please forgive my grammar my fellow readers? I titled this section this because I've realized over the years that it starts with me. See, for years I blamed others for my problems and misfortunes especially my ex-girls, but when I think back I realize that there were always signs that this female wasn't the one. I mean, just look at how and were we met. First there was Jessica Wright who I met at the night club with her home-girls. She was light-skinned with hazel eyes, every weekend when we would come to the club she was always be there dancing all sexy and seductively, but this one night I just couldn't resist. After about three days of kicking it we decided to give this relationship thing a try.

One day while at her house the phone rang, "Hello"?

"Who this"!

"Homie you called my house!"

"Let me speak to Jessica"!

"Who the hell is this", already knowing who he is, but not liking the tone in his voice.

"Her baby daddy punk now put her on the phone"!

"Dre who is that", she asks?

"Your pussy ass baby daddy"

"Forget you homie I bet you won't say that shit to my face!"

"If you show your punk ass face, I'm a punch you in your face you punk ass bitch"!

"Come outside then punk", and then hangs up in my face.

So I put my shoes on and went outside very upset pacing back and forth in the parking lot ready to fight. After about five minutes this green and white car pulls up. Seven brothers got out talking mad shit and formed a circle around me; this punk ass brother couldn't fight one on one he had to bring his boys. I remembered what Big Perm always told me, "Hit the one with the most mouth and talking the most shit", so I turned and punched the one with the biggest mouth; which was her baby daddy. After that punch, his bigger home-boy on my left punched me in the face and I hit the ground. Right as I was trying to get up I saw another one of his home-boys draw back his leg like he was getting ready to kick a football; all of this seemed to be moving in slow motion. He kicked me right in my face and that's all I remembered. When I came to I was in the hospital and they said I had been there for three days. That relationship ended before it ever really got started.

Second there was Stacy Omari; she was half black and Indian. The night we met I'll never forget. Once again it was at the night club, and this particular night the club was really jumping. As we were walking in we were getting mad love and respect from everybody; that's when I noticed her on the other side of the dance floor. She was dancing by herself beside one of her home-girls. I was trying to make eye contact with her for about thirty minutes, but for some reason she wasn't looking back. Her home-girl was the first to notice that I was checking her out. I saw her nudge her and then try to be slick and nudge her in my direction. Then they both start giggling and acting silly.

I get up from the table where I was sitting and walk over to her and say, "Excuse me!" trying to talk over the music.

She turns and looks at me with her beautiful light brown eyes, and then I ask, "Do you want to dance!"

I can tell that she was shy and in a shy like voice she says, "Yes".

I grab her by the hand and lead her to the dance floor. In all honesty, we danced the whole night away with one another. The bond between us would lead to my first born son.

Finally there was the worst woman I had ever met, and been in a relationship with in my whole entire life; Yvette Ruiz. She was a stripper and very, very beautiful. I bet you can't guess where I met her? Yep, you guessed right, I met her at the strip club. She was the main attraction and would always turn it out to. Honestly she was the best looking and dancing female they had; she was originally from Los Angeles. In this case I didn't approach her she approached me and made it clear that she wanted me, but I had a girl at the time and that was Stacy. One night while we were at the strip club she was dancing for me and my homie Deuce.

"A homie I'm about to get this", I say to Deuce while she dances for us.

"Shoot I don't blame you."

I dipped out early that night because I told Stacy I would be home at a decent hour.

The next day the crew was meeting up over Deuce house to do our weed sampling like we always did. This consisted of rolling up about twenty blunts, and allowing all our friends to get high on us, but to my surprise, I see Yvette over here walking around in a short cut sport shirt, and some very tight and short shorts.

"What and the hell is she doing over here, didn't I tell you I was going to holla at that"?

"Oh yea, we talking now"

"Deuce, you don't even know her you shouldn't be sporting her like this at these type of gatherings".

"Dre I got this don't worry about me", and then he walks off.

That whole night she had her eyes on me and I was trying to play it off, but to make a long story short it happen; the split of the Too Real Click.

Two days later Yvette and I started having sex and we kept on doing it for over a month before Deuce even caught on that she was messing around on him.

One day Deuce came by the house with tears in his eyes asking for my help, he says, "Dre I think Yvette is cheating on me and I want you to help me find out who it is."

"No problem homie I got you"

With tears running down his face he says, "I can't believe she would do me like this as good as I've been to her!"

"Don't worry homie as soon as we find out who it is I'm a beat his ass down my self". Knowing the whole time it was me.

The next day she calls me and starts tripping saying, "Dre I want to be with you."

"Yvette calm down let's just take our time".

48

"No, I want to be with you and I can't fight it any longer, I'm a tell Deuce about us."

"No"!

"Oh you want to sex me but you don't want to be with me"?

"It's not that, I just think that's the wrong way of going about it".

"Well I'm telling him and I'm also going to tell Stacy to and then we can be together for real; you do want to be with me right"?

"Yeah", and then we hang up.

When Deuce found out it was me he just couldn't believe it and he was very deeply hurt, along with a few other people in our click. He wouldn't have thought it was me in a million years; needless to say the click broke up. Stacy moved and didn't tell me were she was going. She just took off and until this very day I have never seen my son. Deuce also left Fairbanks and when he left a piece of me left to; this was my homie who would've stuck with me through thick and thin. Other then Perm he was the only one I would've trusted with my life, and now that he was gone things would definitely change and not for the good either, but for the worst. Yvette took me down through there to over the next couple years; the constant arguing and fighting. The constant stealing of my money and weed, the constant cheating and like the Bible says, "We always reap what we sow".

CHAPTER 7
GETTING TURNED ON

RIDING DIRTY (THE SET-UP)

B efore we go any further I just wanted to let yaw know that those brothers that jumped me didn't get away with it? I ran into them again at the club several months later, and when I recognized it was them it was definitely on.

Nudging Perm and pointing towards them with my head I say, "There those dudes that jumped me."

"That's them right there, oh it's on".

"It was seven of them let me look around and see if his homies are here."

After scoping the club out I come back and tell Perm, "They all are here and the one who started this stuff is on the stage dancing".

"Do what you do I have your back".

So I walk up on the stage laying low waiting for the right time. As soon as I felt the time was right I just punched him with a one hitter quitter. We fall off the stage, I land on top of him, and I just kept throwing and landing deadly punches to his face. With my fist all bloody one of his home-boys grab me from behind and puts me in a head lock, but I heard Perm say, "Oh hell naw get your hands off my little brother!"

I guessed he must've punched him because all of a sudden his arms fell off my neck. The club bouncers came and got me off ole boy. When they pulled me off I looked over and seen his other home-boy who helped jump me and I punched his block off and he hit the floor.

Perm and some of the other homies grabbed the bouncers pulling their arms off of me; because I was caught up in the moment I was ready to fight any and every body.

Pulling and pushing the bouncer's arms off me I shout in anger, "Get your hands off me, I'm not scared of none of yaw bitches!"

As I pulled free they still kept leading us out the club. I look over and see the punk ass dude who kicked me in my head, and my last punch was my best one. I hit him so hard I sent him flying over the table they say when he got up he had a swollen face. The next day I seen some people who were their when all this went down, and they was like that was the most excitement they had seen in a long time. I started getting mad props from everybody; everywhere I went. All of a sudden I start getting messages from these punk ass cowards saying they want to call a truce.

So I sent a message back saying, "If you say so."

After the click broke up; all the homies who weren't down with us any more started doing their own thing. Money Kell did a few more weed runs with me after Deuce left, but made it clear that after the last one he was done with me and Perm. He went from helping us move our weed to getting back into the cocaine game. He was doing his thing and we heard he was the man when it came to powder. One night while he was out making a run to make a sell he got pulled over for making an improper lane change, they searched his car, and he went to jail. While he was in jail they questioned him about the weed trade going on from Fairbanks to Anchorage.

"How you know about that!"

"We know about everything Kelvin".

"If you knew everything why did you just ask me about it?"

"Look Kelvin, you facing some time, if you know something give it up and I promise you, you want do more than 3 years".

"What you want to know?"

Money Kell gave up everything he knew and we didn't even know it. Needless to say they were on the weeds trips we were making to Anchorage. Three weeks after all this went down; they made their move and stopped me in Wasilla on a trip headed back to Fairbanks. Truthfully, I was scared as hell and they knew it. They interrogated me the whole night, but I kept giving them the same answer, "I don't know what you're talking about", all I kept doing was denying that I knew anything. They let the dudes that were in the car with me go and only kept me. I just couldn't believe this shit; we had been so careful and always covered our tracks. Now they are threatening me with 15 to 25 years in prison; "Damn what am I going to do now!"

"Standing outside of my childhood church and the wind is blowing really hard. It's blowing so hard it feels like it's trying to blow me away. I'm standing strong refusing to be moved; the next thing I know I'm standing on the front porch of the church. I can vividly see and hear someone speaking in the church, but honestly I'm not sure. What in the world is going on here I'm thinking to myself; I turn around to look behind me, and as I do, all of a sudden, thunder starts rolling really hard and lightening starts flashing from every were. The strong winds start blowing me really hard again, so I fall to my knees with my hands on my face, and I cry out, "Lord please helps me!" All of a sudden calm comes; the winds, and the thunder and lightening stops. I looked up and out of nowhere this shining light appears and starts coming towards me, but as it's coming towards me I notice that it's speeding up. I stand up squinting at this light trying to make sense of it. Than I realize that this light is going to hit me, but it was too late; BOOM!!!"

DOING TIME AND THE CHARGES BEING DROP

After being interrogate very unfairly and unconstitutional for about five hours, the detective who was doing the interrogation had one of the guards come, pat me down, and take me to a holding cell with no outside windows. That night they brought me a foam tray with nasty disgusting food, and milk the size of the milk cartons you would get in elementary school. They would slide these trays through a square slot opening in the big solid door with a thick solid window. They also came and did head counts twice that morning, and when they came they would shout, "Head count! Get up and come to your cell door window and say your name!"

After being in that holding cell for about three days they came and made me strip down and get dressed out in jailhouse attire. From there they took me down this solid concrete and long bright hall way, and brought me to another big solid door but this one had big solid glass windows on it. Once it opened another guard took custody of me and led me to what looked like a security desk. Again they patted me down, and one of the guards gave me a gray basket, and then issued me a towel, a wash cloth, a small bar of soap, a toothbrush and toothpaste, and two covers and a pillow. He then took me inside a block that had four other cells in it. He took me to the third door; he unlocked it, and then pushed me inside the cell. There was already someone in there and honestly I was a little scared and nervous because I didn't know what to expect.

Keeping my back to the door holding my basket I say, "What's up?"

"What's up?"

"Dre", I reply.

"Keith".

I gave him some dap and let me tell you, this guy was a humongous Eskimo. He was about 6'3, 250lbs, and had giant hands.

"So I guess the top bunk is mine"?

"It doesn't matter to me I can sleep wherever".

Thinking to my, "I've never slept on the top bunk before, I'm just going to see how this goes if I say I want the bottom bunk", which he is already sleeping on. Sitting my stuff on the table by the door I say, "You mind if I sleep on the bottom?"

With no hesitation it seemed like he grabs his stuff in one big swipe, and threw it on the top bunk, then starts making his bed. I grab my stuff and goes over to the bottom bunk and start making mine. After he finished his bed he sits on the table and then asks, "What you in for?"

"Drugs and you"

"Hell I violate my probation, and then they gave me 90 days".

"What you on probation for?"

"I have three DUI's, and the third one got me violated".

He then gets up and jumps up on the top bunk, and once he did that, I lied back with my hands behind my head thinking about that has taken place. Closing my eyes, but trying to stay awake I started thinking "What's next". We kept talking doing our best to size up and get to know one another. As it turned out he kind of knew of me from the streets, but as we were talking we both fell asleep and didn't wake up until the morning when breakfast arrives.

What I'm about to describe was the routine that went on in here everyday: They would wake us up for breakfast around six in the morning; which we had to eat in our cells. Around eleven, they would let us out for what they called recreational activities, where we could play cards, dominoes, or watch TV until lunch came; which we received every other day. Dinner always came between five and six; which again we had to eat in our cells. They would let us back out for recreational activities around seven when they picked up the trays, and we would stay out until 11; then they would lock us down again, do a head count, and like I said earlier, we would do it all over again the next day.

Keith and I got real close over his 90 day stay. Since I wasn't from Alaska the District Attorney was afraid I would leave the state (which I would've), so they didn't give me a bond. The guards kept coming to get me every three months to take me back and forth to court, but for some odd reason the judge just kept sending me back to my cell putting off my court date each time. The night before Keith left, I told him to keep his head up and to do the right thing like he promised he would. I thought I would be getting out right behind him because the drug tasks force didn't have all their evidence, but it didn't work out that way. I eventually did have all the charges against me dropped; 16 months later because of lack of evidence. Yes, that's right I did 19 months for nothing. While I was in there I had decided that I was going to move back home whenever I got released, and on July 28th, 1999, I was set free. Big Perm picked me up from the city jail and he wasn't too happy with my decision about going back home, but he took me to the airport, I bought a plane ticket, we smoked weed what seemed to be all night long, and 24 hours later I was on my way back to Knoxville, TN after being gone for six years.

HEADED HOME TO KNOXVILLE, TN

CHAPTER 8
WELCOME HOME

GREETED BY MY MOTHER

"*W*e are now arriving in Knoxville, TN, we ask that you please buckle your seat belts and put your seats in the upright position as we prepare to land*"*, said a calm smooth voice over the intercom.

Usually I'll be sleep at this time because I'm a little scared of heights, but for some reason I'm just too damn excited about coming home I don't know what to do. As the plane starts to land I grab the armrests on my seat and push myself back against my seat really hard. With my eyes shut tight and feeling a little nervous because like I said earlier I would normally be sleep, you all should've heard and seen me praying, "Lord please don't let us crash, please don't let us crash, I'm a do better, please Lord."

As soon as the plane landed and they started letting us file off; you should've seen me, I left a trail of smoke getting off that plane. As I ran down the terminal the first face I seen was my dear sweet mother, and I grabbed her and hugged her like I never had before.

While hugging one another and with tears in her eyes she says, "Welcome home son, welcome home!"

"It feels so good to be back mama!"

We walked to the luggage area, and I got my luggage. On the drive to the house we talked about everything, and she caught me up on what has happen down here in the last six years while I was gone. It felt so good to talk to my mama and be home, and I couldn't wait to see my little brother because we haven't seen one another, nor have we talked in a very long time.

The first thing I did when I got home was eat some good home cooking. I mean, we had fried chicken, pinto beans, corn bread, and collard greens; and it was off the chain to. Next I called Lee and talked to him, and we caught up on some things and made plans to hook up tomorrow. It was weird at first because when I left he was a 14 year old immature kid; now he's a 20 year old mature grown man. I called my dad and let him know that I had made it into town; I called him simply because we stayed in touch over the years. I let go of the fact that he wasn't in our lives when we were young, even though my brother never has. Finally, I went to my room to lie down and got me some rest because I had jet lag and was tired. It felt like I slept for three days straight; everybody kept coming by wanting to see me, but I was just too tired to talk. Big Perm even called and I was so tired I couldn't even remember what we talked about. After I finally woke up I went down stairs to get me something to drink; as I walked in, my mama was at the kitchen table watching her soaps; she hasn't changed a bit.

"So what are you going to do now that you home?"

"What you mean"?

"When are you going to get off your lazy butt and start looking for a job?"

"Dang mama I just got here, I'm hooking up with Lee Thursday, and he told me that he knew a few places that were hiring, than I'm a meet up with daddy Friday, and I'll ask him to run me around to a few places, momma trust me, I have everything under control".

I give her a kiss on the cheek, and as I walk away I'm thinking "Oh God here we go with this", I already knew what lied ahead. Needless to say my home warming ended before it even got started, and finding a job just wasn't that easy. As I sit here thinking and looking back I wonder; did I really apply my self?

CAN'T FIND A JOB, SO MOVES IN WITH DAD

For some reason I thought finding a job was going to be a whole lot easier, I mean, I was going every where on the bus, and I was willing to do anything. One place I went to wanted more of a work history; another I felt like they didn't hire me because I was black. Besides all that I had to come home and hear my dear sweet mama's loud ass mouth.

"Have you found a job yet"!

"No ma'am, and I've been everywhere to".

Sitting up on the couch she says with an attitude, "I just don't believe that, I'm starting to get the impression that you don't want to work".

"Now why you say that?"

"Because you not working, and it's been two months since you so-called been looking".

I can't lie, that remark really hurt my feelings, so as I hold back my pain and tears I say, "Mama trust me I've been trying", then I ran up the stairs and went to my room. This scenario went for about two more weeks, but enough was enough I just couldn't take it anymore. So I packed up my stuff and moved in with my dad, against my mama's will.

My dad drove a red Dodge Dakota truck, with sporty white stripes on the side, and very shiny chrome wheels; I can't lie that was a pretty truck. When he picked me up I could tell from the look in his eye's that he was really excited about this. We stopped and had lunch at a local diner as I explained the situation between my mother and me.

"Son what's going on with you and your mama"?

"Man I don't know, it just seemed as if she don't believe in me."

The waitress comes up and we order our food then he says to me, "Well you need someone to believe in you; because when you do that helps keep you motivated".

"Dad, it just wasn't as easy as I thought it was going to be".

"Son if it comes easy; trust me you don't want it".

That comment kind of put me in deep thought, and he could tell, so then he says, "But we not going to worry about that right now, we going to focus on some eating, and then go home smoke a fat one", and that's how we ended that conversation.

After three weeks of looking for a job, I finally found one at the Living Assisting Center. At this program we helped mentally challenged people with their everyday activities; such as: Bathing, shopping, and cooking. Honestly, I loved my job, but the truth was; it wasn't paying me enough. I mean check this out: I bought a car, I had to pay half the rent and utilities, and my dad and I had habits or better yet a habit; (WEED). Most of my money went to buying my weed, and when you don't make enough to pay your bills and support your habit, well; you do what you have to do to get high. Trust me, it's nothing like a crack head trying to get high, but I did have my ways; for example: I would leach, meaning I hung around people who smoked. Once the weed was gone so was I, or I would say I was going to match a blunt; which is when you smoke your weed with me, I'm suppose to turn around and smoke my weed with you, but I knew I didn't have any to match. When the blunt got to a certain point, I would be like "I'll be right back", but I never did. These are just a few ways that I would use to get high when I didn't have any, and I know I'm not the only one that pulled these kinds of stunts when it came to getting high?

I've even tried selling weed to, but when you selling by depending on another dealer, you just won't make as much money as you should. This again was frustrating me because I was use to making big money, but wait a minute; what's stopping me from doing here what I did in Alaska? Uh oh, it's about to be on now; I have a plan and I'm a spring it on my dad to see what he thinks. Because if we made a lot of money in Alaska, imagine how much I could make down here.

CHAPTER 9
GETTING BACK ON MY FEET

PUTTING MY PLAN IN MOTION

Like I said in the previous chapter I had a plan, and when I broke it down to my dad he was all for it. Allow me to explain what my plan was: I was going to rent a one bedroom apartment in West Knoxville, not in my name, but in someone else's. In this place I was going to set up the bedroom as a grow room where I would plant about sixteen plants removing all the males as soon as I recognize them. I had to burn incenses constantly because of the very strong skunk smell the plants were producing. I would stay at the apartment from time to time just so I could be seen and not draw any unnecessary suspicion. I went to work everyday just like I normally did, occasionally stopping by checking on my plants. It seemed like the three months required for growing weed took for ever, but when it came I was there just about half the night pulling them up and getting them ready. I would take a couple of clothes basket with clothes in them to the apartment, but when I left; it would just be clothes on the top. I took a couple of plants still on the stalk to my daddy's house, and he fell in love with them. I actually gave him a couple of buds still on the branch. What he loved most about my weed just like every one else will, was the fact of little or no seeds. We smoked a couple of joints and where high out of our minds; we laughed all night long and ate up everything in the house.

The next day I was all about my business, I worked through the night the whole weekend trying to get my weed right. In Alaska it was me and Perm, here it's just me. I mean, I know it's only sixteen plants, but you have to make sure everything is done right. I had to take one of the plants and dedicate that one to cloning, and I had to make sure all the unused stuff was disposed of properly. It might sound easy, but trust me; it's not as easy as it sounds.

After all the work was done and I had my weed bagged up. I drove to my dad's house to show him the finish product.

"What's up Milton you got everything ready to go I see?"

"Hell finally, it took me this whole weekend to get all this stuff ready."

"Well how much do you have"?

So I take all the baggies out the basket, and he was like, "DAMN!"

"I have 250 baggies weighed at 3 grams, which I'm a sell at ten dollars a piece".

"That's a lot of weed, and a lot of money, so be careful."

"Dad trusts me I got this".

"I know you do son."

"Matter of fact here's a few baggies just in case you know someone looking for some".

I want to make him feel special because in actuality he is. I say this because if it wasn't for him, this wouldn't even be possible.

Now that I have the easy part over with; now it's time to put plan B into action; which is the hardest part. I guess you probably asking yourself, "What's the hardest part?" The hardest part is getting the clientele.

STARTING OUT SLOW, BUT THEN BLOWING UP

Everyday when I got off work I would go straight to the hood and just park and post up in front of my mama's apartment. For some reason nobody would even stop and fool with me. I guess when people have their certain dealers that they fool with, once their minds made up that that person has the best; they won't fool with anyone else. Because I been sitting out in this car day and night, rain or snow for about two weeks now, and when I tell somebody, "I got that green", they act like they don't even hear me.

In my heart I feel like giving up, but I know I really need this money; what can I do to put myself out their I think to myself? Then it hit me, this is all profit, I can afford to smoke a few sacks with people, so they can see what I have to offer. So I changed up my game; instead of coming to the hood and setting up to post, I started rolling up with some of the homies from the hood that I knew since I was little, and that I knew smoked weed.

"What's up Travis, you want to smoke this blunt with me", I asked as I'm sitting on the steps, in front of my mama's apartment with the blunt in my mouth. Already knowing where he's headed; to the weed man or woman, but on the real, who in the hell is going to turn down a free high?

He kind of hesitated, leaned up against the fence, and with a surprised look and shocked in his voice, he says, "Hell yeah!" See in the hood brothers just didn't do things like that.

I take the blunt out my mouth, fire up the lighter, placing the end of the blunt to be fired up in the flame, and then I start sucking on the blunt; inhaling some of the smoke and blowing some of it out. When the sweet potent skunk smell hit the air I could see that Travis eye's lit up; I already know down here they haven't had anything like this before. I say this because Perm and I became weed doctors; we knew how to make our weed plants produce THC real strong and good.

"Damn cuz where you get your weed from"! Looking at him I could tell he couldn't wait for me to pass it to him, so I did.

"Homie make sure you take it easy this weed isn't no joke", but before I could get it out he hits the blunt too hard and coughs like he's getting ready to cough up a lung.

With a sneaky smile on my face I pat him the back a couple times and say, "I tried to warn you".

Trying to catch his breath he says, "Where can I get some of this at"?

"What you looking for"?

"I want a dub"

Passing the blunt back to him I say, "Take it easy this time when you hit it, and yeah I got you but I only have dime sacks."

"That's cool".

"Come over to the car and I got you".

I get in on the driver's side and he get's in on the passenger side, and then I gave him two dime sacks.

"Make sure you let everybody know that I have that fire".

"I got you, how long you going to be right here"?

Checking the time on my car radio I say, "I'll be here for a minute".

He leaves headed up the street as soon as I get out the car one of the home-girl's from the neighborhood named Kamisha comes up to me and says, "Is that skunk weed you smoking on?"

"Yeah, what's up"?

Walking up real close on me she says, "I want a half O".

"I only have dime sacks, and if it's cool with you I'll give you six for fifty even though I know you getting me".

Wasting no time she says, "Deal"!

"Follow me this way", I reply walking towards my car. We get in and make the transaction.

"You have a number so I can contact you"? At the time I didn't, but I knew my dad did, so I gave her his number and then she got out and went her way.

On this night I made $150, but the next night I sold out of everything I had. That's because I would only keep $500 worth of weed on me at a time. It started out slow, but after a month I was the man in the hood to see when you wanted some fire ass weed. Now people would wait for me when they wanted to buy weed. I sold out of that first crop I planted, but the next crop was only a matter of weeks away. The game was definitely changing up and I was clearing easily a $1000 a week after the next crop came in. I increased my operation and started producing more, so guess what I had to do? I had to quit my job, I know it sounds stupid, but I felt like the money was worth it. My dad gave me his cell phone because everyone that called it was calling for me, and I bought him a new one, hell I was booming. I would post in two hoods now; I was trying to make all the money I could. One day while posting on the east side my cell phone rings, it's Big Perm, "What's up big homie everything ok"?

CHAPTER 10
OPERATION # 2

BIG PERM AND DRE BACK TOGETHER AGAIN

"**M**an, this girl up here tripping", he shouts through the phone!

"Who"!

There's a short pause between us, but I could hear him saying something muffled to somebody. "Perm what's going on"!

"Fine then, if that's what you want, that's what you get", he shouts and then she shouted something back at him; I could tell it was a woman's voice, but I couldn't make out what she was saying.

With frustration and anger in his voice, he shouts through the phone, "Dre this girl done accused me of cheating on her, saying that one of her co-workers claim that we are messing around"!

"Who is she"!

"Some girl name Maya", he shouts! Now to be honest, Perm does mess with this girl, but I know he doesn't want to lose his family so I play alone.

"Damn homie that's messed up".

"Dre, this bitch done caused me to lose my family and I'm not too happy about it"!

Trying to do my best to calm my big homie down, I say, "Perm you know Denise not going to let you go any where".

"Man she already got my shit backed up"!

"For real", I ask with surprise in my voice, because this time I am surprised!

"Hell yeah"!

I paused for a moment because I'm kind of shocked by all this, "So what you going to do"?

"Shit I don't know, hell if she don't want me here what am I suppose to do", he ask with sadness in his voice. I feel his pain, they have a young daughter together and I personally know how hard it is to leave your baby behind when you really don't want to.

"Perm, is there not anyway you and her can work this out"?

He pauses for a moment and I can hear him crying in the background, he says, "Dre she had all my stuff packed up when I got home from work, it's clear she doesn't want me here, she won't even let me see my daughter or tell my side of the story".

"What you need me to do homie"?

He pauses for a moment, and then says, "Can I come and stay with you for a little while"?

"That's no problem, you know I got you".

Now this was definitely unexpected I just knew he was going to go back home to Virginia.

"I won't be there too long, just long enough to get my head together".

"That's cool, how are you going to get down here"?

After he takes a deep breathe, he says, "I guess I'm a drive down there".

"Damn Perm that's a long ass drive, why don't you just fly"?

"Because I don't want to leave my studio equipment behind"

"So when are you going to leave out"?

I can hear him calculating through the phone, and then he says, "I guess I'm a leave out tomorrow."

"Damn, why so soon"?

With pain in his voice, he says, "The sooner the better". So I ended the conversation on that note.

"You want me to fly up and drive out with you"?

"Naw, I got it, I'll be fine".

I take a deep breathe, and then say, "I'll be listening out for you big homie, have a safe trip".

Eighteen days later after Perm did all his sight seeing in the state of Washington, California, Colorado, and Texas. He called me when he got in Nashville, and then I knew he wasn't too far away. When he arrived in Knoxville I met him at the King of Burgers restaurant on Kingston Pike, I just couldn't believe it; my big brother and I where back together again. After we met up, we went to an all you can eat buffet where I broke down to him what I've been up to since being back home and he was down with the plan. I think all my bragging over the next two weeks made him decide that he wanted to stay.

"Do you know where I can find a cheap place"?

Not saying anything until we stopped at the up coming stop light, I say, "What"!

"I've decided to stay Dre".

Thinking he's joking, I respond with a sarcastic, "Really now".

"Dre I'm dead serious, I like it here and plus we can watch each other's back like old times".

I'm feeling that statement, so then I say, "It all depends on what you define as being cheap".

"About $600.00 a month"

Looking at him like he's crazy, I say, "We not in Alaska anymore Toe-Doe, down here in Tennessee the cost of living is a whole lot cheaper.

He then holds his hand out to give me some dap and says, "So does this mean you got me"?

"Shoot, I can fine you nice ass apartment for that price big homie".

After three weeks of staying with me, Perm finally got his own place, and he set it up the same way he did back in Alaska; I mean, with the studio. We then teamed up and started back selling weed together. I kept the spot down west were I was growing the weed and gave him a key to it. Shit, I already know it's going to be on and popping now. This meant that whenever I posted up on the east or west side of town, my big homie was right there with me. I introduced him to my mama, daddy, and little brother and they treated him like he was part of the family. It was just like old times; me and Big Perm making big money again, but I think it took him some getting use to when he heard everybody calling me by my real name "Milton"; because he never called me that.

MEETING UP WITH MY LITTLE HOMIE CHEESE

Last night after a night of clubbing, smoking weed, drinking, and making money; I had Big Perm drop me off at this girl's house that I met a few weeks ago at the club. We had met up a couple times since than; at the store and at laundry mat. We had talked about five or six times on the phone since we first met, so I wasn't surprised when she told me before I went out to stop by her place afterwards. This wasn't the first time a female had came at me like this, so I already knew what to expect. Deep down in my heart, I knew she wasn't about nothing but money, but in my eyes she was beautiful as hell and plus I wanted her real bad. When I got to her place, I knocked on the door, and she opened it in her night robe. She was laughing and I noticed her watching "Friday after Next", so I sat down on the couch she was sitting on and started rolling up a couple of blunts. She had candles burning and the house smelled like fresh lavender. I could also tell that she had on some kind of sweet and seductive smelling perfume, simply, she smelled so damn good. After we smoked the first blunt and the skunk smell of the weed filled the air, I could feel that she wanted to get this party started, so I said to her, "Why you sitting way over there, slide a little closer so I can hold you?"

"My bad, I didn't want to make you feel uncomfortable", she replies as she slides a little closer and I put my arms around her. I grab the second blunt and fired it up, and by the time it was half way gone she was all over me. I mean, we started kissing like two wild animals. The lustful attraction had both of us ready to burst. She pulled my shirt off of me and I slid her robe off of her. She had on nothing and her body looked so damn perfect, soft, and smooth. Her breast were just the right size with perfectly round nipples and her pussy was shaved and well kept, so I laid her back on the couch and start licking and sucking on her clique and pussy. This drove her crazy and I could feel and taste that she came like three times in my mouth, but hell I didn't care. Once I knew I had her wanting it, I carried her to the bedroom, took off my pants and boxers, and put my hard big cock in her tight wet pussy, and it was on. Needless to say, your boy put it down, but after I hit it a couple of times and she was sound asleep, I was ready to go.

I went to the bathroom a couple of times trying to call Perm so he could come and get me, but I couldn't reach him. I left a couple of messages hoping that he would respond sooner rather then later, but he never did. So I went back to the bedroom and just laid there on the bed, with my hands behind my head, looking up at ceiling. I looked over at her alarm clock and it read 4:47 a.m., but I must've dosed off because the next time I looked at the clock it read 6:13 a.m. As I'm staring at the ceiling a beam of sunlight sneaks through the blinds and hits me in my face. When I turned over on my side, to escape the beam of sunlight that was hitting me in my face, I noticed that she was staring right at me with a big ass smile on her face.

"Did you get any sleep", she asks?

"A little", right than my phone started ringing, thinking that it's Perm I answer it like, "its about damn time Homie!"

The woman's voice on the other end replies, "Damn, did I call at the wrong time?"

"Who this"?

"Kierra"

"Oh, my bad, I thought you were someone else, what's up"?

"I need to holla at you as soon as possible".

"Same thing"

"Yeah"

"I'll be there in a minute", and I hang up.

As soon I hung up with her I called Big Perm again and this time he answers in his just woke up voice, "What's up you ready?"

"Homie I've been ready, I have business I need to tend to".

"I'm on my way", so we hang up and I sat up on the edge of the bed and started putting my clothes on.

"So you getting ready to go"

"Yeah baby I have some business I need to take care of".

"When we going to kick it again"?

"When do you want to"?

"Shit, tonight".

"Then tonight it is, and this time I'm a drive my own car". A horn blows, we give one another a hug, she sneaks in a kiss, and then I left.

"Can you run me to the Westside I need to holla at somebody", I shout as I'm approaching the car. He was smoking a blunt and passed it to me when I shut the door, and then we pulled off. On the ride over there I was getting everything ready to make a deal.

We pulled up at Kierra apartment and she was standing outside waiting on me. She gets in and says, "What's up Milton, it took you long enough".

"I was a little busy when you called, but you know I keep that fire".

"That's why I waited on you".

I passed her what was left of the blunt we were smoking, she gave me the fifty dollar bill, and I gave her the half ounce of weed.

She smelled it and then said, "Damn homie this shit smell fire as hell"!

"You already know I don't mess with nothing, but the best".

"Milton can you do me a favor"?

"What's up"?

"My cousin is trying to find an ounce of some fire ass weed, I told him I knew someone, but that I had to make sure it was cool with you first".

"He cool"

"Hell yeah I know you'll like him".

"Where does he stay"?

"Over in the Fields".

"Call and tell him we own our way".

She dials his number and tells him we are on our way, I give her some dap, and then we rolled out.

Her cousin's name was Eugene, and she was right he was cool as hell. After he bought that first ounce from us for $100, he kept buying them at least three times a day over a three week time period. Perm became curious and wanted to know what he was doing, so the next time we met up with him, Perm just asked him, "How you making this money so fast"?

"Man I just bag up twelve baggies; sell them at ten dollars a piece, I take the $100 buy another ounce from yaw, and I pocket the twenty".

"Damn don't you think that that's backwards hustling homie?"

"Shit that's all that I can afford right now".

"So what, you wanting to make some real money", I ask?

"Shit, hell yeah"!

"Perm, let's take a drive".

"Dre what you doing"!

"Perm this man is making that cheese, and if he had the right connect he probably could make a whole lot more, think about it".

He pauses for a moment, and then says, "Yeah you right".

We rode to my apartment, and I gave Eugene eight ounces, and told him to go hit the block and make that money. By the end of the week this brother brought us $850 back, and we split it with him.

"Eugene, welcome to the team, and if you don't mind me saying, your new name is Cheese".

"Why you say that"?

"Because you be making that Cheese", Big Perm replied!

Once he came aboard and helped us move our weed. Our production and money making happily increased, and it was on. Oh, yeah, me and ole girl did hook up later that night, and we still kicked it from time to time, but you can't tie a player like me down; shit that's what I do, and being tied down just isn't me; so I thought.

GIRL OF MY DREAMS

One Thursday night Big Perm decided to have a little house party at his place. The plan was to get high; on weed of course, drink some beer and/ or liquor; which ever you prefer, and sit in the studio and mess around. So I asked Perm to run me by the grocery store so I could pick up a few cases of beer, because the beer in the grocery store is a whole lot cheaper then at the gas station. As I was walking to the beer aisle, I passed the potatoes' chip aisle, and the girl in that aisle was so damn fine I had to do a double take. She had a caramel complexion, about 5'3 and 125 pounds, with beautiful brown eyes, her body was shaped perfectly, and as she reached up to grab a bag of chips I could see that she had an awesome mid-section. I couldn't see her hair because she had a red scarf on, and allow me to be honest with yaw; the shape of her perfectly round booty is what caught my attention. I stood at the front of the aisle acting like I was looking at the laundry detergent, but I was thinking if I should approach her or not. I mean, I was a handsome young man, I had taste, plus I was clean to death. Forget it, the worst she could say is "No"; Luther Vandross told us to at least try.

As I walked towards her I kind of got the feeling she knew I was checking her out because she really wasn't trying to leave, so I say to her, "Excuse me, where do I know you from?"

"I don't know, I don't think I've ever seen you before".

"You sure because you look so very familiar, I know where it was, at the night club".

"Nope wasn't me, because I don't go to the club".

"Ok, it's clear that I don't know you, but is it ok if I get to know you"?

She starts smiling and acting like she wanted to walk away, so I say, "Look here's my number, why don't you give me call if you want to get to know one another".

"Really, you sure you don't have a woman and how you know I don't have a man"?

"If you had a man would you be standing here talking to me; you mind if I walk you to the check out"?

Cracking a little smile, she replies, "I don't mind."

Holding my hand out introducing myself I say, "My name is Dre, what's yours?"

She shakes it and replies, "Juliet."

"Juliet, what a beautiful name, I hope some day I can be your Romeo".

Blushing and attempting to change the subject she asks, "What you doing tonight?"

"Why you ask that"?

"Because you all dressed up and looking good".

"Thank you, you also looking really damn good yourself; my friend is having a little get together at his place; he has a studio and we be messing around just acting silly, do you smoke"?

"I don't smoke cigarettes, but I definitely smoke weed".

"Because a little of that's going to be going on to, and you welcome to come"

"You gave me your number now I'm giving you mine; 555-8763."

"Do you want to come tonight?"

"Maybe"

"If you don't feel comfortable coming by yourself bring a friend or two with you".

"What time are yaw getting started"?

"We headed that way now; I'm calling you so you will have my number in your phone, you can throw that piece of paper away".

"O.k., I'll call you if I decide to come".

We said our good byes and I walked to the car. As soon as I sat down I realized that I forgot to get the beer, so I had to run back in the store and get it.

Later that night Juliet and her two cousins did come over, and we got tore up to. We all were so messed up that nobody could drive home. After that day Juliet and I spent a lot of time with one another. We kicked it for two weeks before we even had sex, and the sex was banging. She didn't trip when she found out what I did for a living; she actually turned us on to a few more big spenders. If you don't mind allow me to tell you all what I liked about this girl. She had a good attitude, she wasn't loud and ghetto, she dressed with class, she kept her hair and nails done, and she always seemed to have my back no matter what it was; in my heart I just felt like she was the right one for me. My family loved her and her family loved me. We decided to become a serious couple after a month of dating. Three months into the relationship she became pregnant and nine months later we had a son. Even though all this positive stuff came with Juliet I just wouldn't quit what I was doing, I mean, I still messed around. So my question to yaw is this: "How come we can have a good thing going, but for some reason we always find a way to mess it up?" If you know, get back at me.

CHAPTER 11
A ROBBERY

SLIPPING HARD AND THEN SET UP

One very cold Tuesday morning while I was in the kitchen fixing me and Juliet some breakfast, my cell phone rings, "Hello"?

"Can I speak to Milton"?

"Who is this"?

"Arsenio"!

"Man I know who you are, what's up"?

"I need to come down their and holler at you".

"When you plan on being here"?

"Friday if that's ok with you".

"Friday it is, I'll see you then", and then we hung up.

Arsenio is my cousin from New York home boy, who I do business with behind my cousin's back. He would always come down about every other month on the Greyhound bus, and buy five pounds at a time. My cousin and I did business to, but you know me, I'm trying to make all the money that I can. Hell, honestly I was greedy and didn't care who I burnt in the process. If Charles knew, no doubt he would be pissed off, but I didn't care, because I run this weed shit right now.

When I picked him up at the bus station I already knew what he wanted to do. He wanted to go to the mall first, stop and get something to eat at a buffet, and then go to the strip club and watch some booty shaking. So as planned we head to the mall, and when we get there we noticed that the parking lot was jam packed, and we couldn't find anywhere to park; we finally did about five minutes later all the way in the back of the lot. We started getting excited, because we already know when it's packed like this; it's mostly going to be females. I notice out the corner of my eye that he couldn't wait to go in, but I know this dude and all he's doing right now is talking bull shit; what he's going to get, and who he's going to holler at. See, I already know he isn't about to do anything, especially when it comes to talking to females, and like always it's going to be all on me to do the pulling.

After we go into a couple stores an buy a couple of things we decided to go to the food court to get something to eat. While we were sitting down eating Arsenio noticed on the other side of the food court that there were a couple of girls trying to get our attention.

"Milton, why don't you go over there and see what's up"?

Giving him a look like no you didn't, I reply, "I thought you were going to do the pulling, that's what you said in the car".

"I know, but I'm a little nervous".

Shaking my head out of disbelief, I reply, "Take notes and watch the master at work".

The only reason I'm doing this is because these three girls are fine as hell. As I approached there table, they were like, "It's about time, what took you so long"!

"Damn my bad, I had to make sure it was us you were looking at".

"What's up with you and your homie"?

"Shoot we were trying to see what's up with yaw".

"Hell I don't have a man".

"Me either".

The other girl didn't say anything so I said, "What about you"?

"I'm not a hot ass like these two, if you want to know if I have a man you have to find out yourself".

Honestly, I like that response so I reply, "Then I guess I'm going to find out". She smiles and then takes a sip from her drink.

"Why don't you sit down", so I have a seat. The girl on the inside starts motioning to Arsenio to come over, and you should've seen the big ass grin on his face.

"My name's Charlene".

"I'm Toni, with an "I".

"And I'm Shea".

"I'm Dre and this is my homie from New York Arsenio."

We talked for about another fifteen minutes, before the subject of playing some spades, drinking some liquor, and smoking some weed came up.

"Shoot I'm down, what time is the ass kicking starting".

"If there's going to be any ass kicking it going to be me and my home girl".

So Shea and I exchange numbers, and I tell her, "I'll call you when we on our way, and you can give me directions then".

I told Arsenio that I had to stop by the house first because I'm about to go all out for these girls, and plus we can go ahead and take care of our business at the same time, but as soon as I come through the door the drama starts.

"Where the fuck you been! I've been calling you all day"!

"Baby chill out, you know I've been taking care of business, you act like you don't know what I do".

"My cousin said she seen your car parked up on Bethel Avenue earlier today, what where you doing over there"!

"What the hell are you talking about"!

"You fucking around with Crystal again aren't you"!

"Juliet, what are you talking about? See there you go assuming again, why do you do that"?

"Milton I want to know the truth, are you"!

"Am I what"?

"Don't play dumb, you know what I'm talking about".

"Baby answers this for me, who am I with you or your cousin"?

"You with me"

"Do you trust me"?

"Yes".

I gives her a kiss on the lips, and then says, "I would never cheat on you baby; people are just jealous of our relationship can't you see that? Don't allow your friends or family to put things in your head that you already know isn't true. Chill out, I'm a go take care of my homie and I'll be back in a few, o.k."?

"O.k. baby"

I run to the closet in the room and get what I need to get, so I can do what I need to do, I give her a long passionate kiss, I kiss my son, and then I dipped out putting a half pound of weed in my coat, and another six pounds in my trunk.

Over at Shea's apartment; which was in the projects, it was going down. They had beer and liquor, and I brought the weed. After about an hour, and after being a little messed up; I take the half pound of weed that I had in my coat and just through it on the table. I also had three boxes of sweet cigars and through them on the table as well, and everybody just started rolling up. I noticed her home girl Toni leaving, but I didn't pay it much attention at the time. Everyone started firing up there blunts and the very potent smell of skunk weed filled the air. The kitchen was so damn smoky that we could hardly see one another, and we were so damn high everyone dosed off and I mean we were knock out sitting at the kitchen table. Next thing I know I hear a door slam and I jump up; the girls were gone, so I woke Arsenio up and told him I was ready to go. I look at the clock on my phone and it says 4:28 a.m. I know I'm in trouble now, so not thinking I just grab my stuff, wake Arsenio up again, and we take off out the door.

When we get to the car I reach in my coat to get my keys and they weren't there. So I started searching my front and back pants pockets and I found them in my left pocket, but I dropped them as I pulled them out my pocket. Arsenio was so messed up that he could hardly stand up, but when I reached down to get my keys off the pavement I felt something cold come against the back of my head.

As I turn my head slightly to see what was going on, I heard a voice say, "Don't move mutherfucka or I'll blow your got damn head off "!

What the hell I thought to myself, and then it dawned on me; I was being robbed.

"Now, I want you to come up slowly and keep your hands where I can see them".

"A homie . . ."?

He stopped me in mid sentence, "Shut the fuck up punk ass bitch, where is the money and weed"!

"Man I don't know what you're talking about", but just then I felt what seemed like a brick hitting me in my head and I hit the pavement, but it was the butt of the sawed off rifle he held in his arms.

As I was trying to get myself up he rushed over to where I was with the barrel of his rifle pointed at me and says, "Look I'm a kill your bitch ass if you don't tell me were the weed and money is"!

Suddenly he grabbed me and I could tell that it was now two of them, and they basically snatched my jack off. Holding my head and with blood pouring down from the cut, I peeked up and noticed that it was four of them all together.

But I've had enough, so I ask, "Where are my keys"?

One of them throws me the keys and I barley caught them. I fumbled around for a second and found the key I was looking for. I put the key in the trunk key slot and opened the trunk. Once I did I heard one them say, "This is it, let's go".

"How much money is it"?

"Eight stacks".

"O.k. let's get out of here, but before we leave"!

I was punched and staggered around on my feet, and then he punched me again, and made sure I fell to the ground. Once I did they started beating and stomping me and I thought they were going to kill me. I got hit with the butt of the rifle again, and then his other home boy jumped in and started pistol whipping me; so I just curled up in a ball. When they finished beating on me I heard a loud crack, and a few stomps, and then Arsenio hit the ground. All I heard after Arsenio hit the ground were running foot steps on the pavement, so I just laid there for a minute trying to get myself together.

"Arsenio, are you o.k."?

"Yeah I'm o.k.", he mumbled back.

By using the car as leverage I struggle to make it to my feet. I struggle over to where Arsenio was and helped him to his feet. To my surprise there was no one in sight that could help us. Gathering myself I grab my keys up off the pavement and unlocked the doors to the car. Arsenio got in and I started it up and backed out of my spot, as I was pulling off Arsenio said, "You sure you alright? You don't look too good".

Feeling kind of woozy I say, "What you mean?" Right then I got very dizzy and lost consciousness and ran into a utility pole. When I came to I was in the hospital on a hospital bed with an oxygen mask on my face; when I looked around I saw my mama, daddy, brother, Perm, Cheese, and Juliet. Everyone had a worried look on there face, and then my dad said, "Do you know how lucky you are to still be alive." I just laid back and closed my eye's thinking about what he just said.

Later it came out that I was set up. The girl Shea that lived there didn't live there anymore when I went over there. There were rumors on the streets on who could've robbed me, but I left that all alone. Because I came back even harder then before; I might be bruised up, I might be scared up, I might even have marks on me that will never go away, but I'm still here. I still sold in that neighborhood and I dared anyone to try something. Arsenio left and I never heard from him again, but it's all good he didn't stop my cash flow and neither did the dudes that robbed me.

CHAPTER 12
PARTYING OUT OF CONTROL

THIS IS THE LIFE; AN ALL WHITE PARTY

As I 'm riding down the street in my brand new car that I just bought with Juliet, I look in my rear view mirror, and start thinking to myself about the life that I've built; and you know what? It's been a pretty damn good one to. What we did in Alaska can't even compare to the business that we're doing now. We were making so much money that all of our families were living very well. I had a house built out in the county and put it in my mama's name, and I also bought a couple of houses around the city and but those in my father's name. I decided to move my grow room from the apartment down west, and put it in a house that was under a fake name. When I made this move we were able to produce more then before, and we were expanding into the surrounding counties and states. Who would've ever thought that it was this much money to be made selling weed? Not me, and alone with our success you know came hating. Why, I don't know, because I showed love to everyone. All my women were living well, and I had three outside of Juliet; that didn't want for anything. Big Perm kept adding more and more stuff to his studio, and his beats were getting tighter and better. We dropped a couple of songs together and he wanted us to focus on the music thing because we sounded real good, but I just wasn't with it; selling and smoking weed was my thing and I felt like I was pretty damn good at it. Cheese finally was able to make a better life for him and his girl. He came up so hard most people didn't even recognize him anymore, but what I liked about him was that he was a true and loyal partner.

I stashed away a lot of big money and didn't let anyone know I was doing it, nor where I was putting it; not even my mama and daddy. My brother was in college and I made sure he didn't want for anything, when ever he wanted something he knew who to come to. See for me, it was all about taking care of my family, but at the same time I had to protect my family. Because if someone wanted to get to me, I just knew they would try to attack the ones I love most. So I posted up look-out soldiers who would step in at a drop of a dime and protect them when need be.

One night Perm and I stopped by the local mom and pop store on the east side of town to buy a couple of beers. After we got them and went up front to pay for them, the owner of the night club "It's going down", whose name was Doc came in.

"I've been looking for you brothers all over town for about a week, where have you two been", he asked sounding like he's almost out of breathe.

"Shit where we always are", Perm replied.

"If you haven't seen us around you must not have been looking too hard", I give the cashier a ten for the beers.

"Look, here you go".

"What's this"?

As I hand the paper to Perm Doc says, "This is a VIP invitation to the all white party at the club Friday night."

"An all white party"!

"Yea, only the local best and ballers are going to be there, and I want you two to be my special guest".

"Man you tripping you don't even know us".

"Like hell I don't, everyone knows about you two".

When he said that I didn't like it and a funny feeling came over me that made me snap, "What the hell you mean by that"!

"Nothing homie, I just want you two to be my guest".

I look at Perm and he looks at me, then Perm says, "If you knew us, you would know that there are three of us."

Holding up both his hands in a peace gesture, he says, "That's cool, I just want the top notch brothers there, and I believe you two are top notch", and then he holds out his hand to give us some dap.

We gave him some dap, and then I said, "We'll be there", and then we went our separate ways.

We told Cheese and he was all hyped up just like a little kid. The next two days we spend a lot of time at the mall, and bought nothing but the best. When we hit the scene, we hit it hard, and heads where definitely turning. Cheese had just bought himself a new car, so we decided to ride in his. He had a candy apple red, sitting up on twenty inch rims, thump in the trunk bad ass ride. We didn't turn the music all the way up because I decided I wanted to sit in the back and be chauffeured. When we pulled up about a half a block away we noticed that they had valet parking. So we pulled up and stopped in front of the club where the valet was. When we got out the car the light hit our platinum Rolex watches and bracelets just right. Our platinum necklaces were swinging and reflecting as we were walking in the club, everyone was taking notice. We were G'ed up and we got a whole lot of love as we walked in through the crowd of people standing on the walls talking. I think we slapped hands and bumped chest with over 200 people before we even got to our table. Doc greeted us when we peeked through the crowd, he came up to us gave us some dap and showed us to our table; and we had nothing but the best at our table. The women were everywhere and they just flocked to us as we sat down.

Perm leans over to me and says, "So this is an all white party."

"Shit, I guess."

Cheese pops the top on the bottle at the table and pours each of us a glass. We raise our glasses up, and then I gave a short but sweet toast, "To the new too real click", they repeated it; we touched glasses and took our drinks. Right after that I pulled out a cigar case, took one of the cigars out, and fired it up. The smell of skunk weed filled the air and surpassed the smell of cigarette smoke and bad weed. Soon after that, all the women were flocking to our table asking to have a seat, and as fine as these women were we couldn't tell them no. Honestly, we lived it up that night. We brought $20, 000 just to blow, and that's what we did. That night for me was all about dressing and impressing. I can't lie; Perm and I took a couple of the girls at the club that night to the Marriott. We damn near fucked their brains out; afterwards we gave them 2 g's a piece, exchanged phone numbers, and then sent them on their way. Even though we sent them on there way the sex didn't end on that night we still messed around from time to time.

As I staggered up to the door of my apartment at 7:30 in the morning, I knew there wasn't going to be much sleeping but a lot of fussing and cussing; and I'm so, so tired. The reason why she is going to be fussing and cussing is because I ignored her texts and phone calls all night long. So I take my keys out my pocket, takes a few deep breaths, unlock and slowly open the door, and I wasn't disappointed.

GETTING MAD RESPECT

After that night, if people hadn't taken notice yet, trust me they are now. Everywhere I went people would come at me like, "Hook me up", and I really wasn't feeling that at all. For example: One day I pulled up on the block making a transaction with one of my little homies, but before we could take care of business some dude walked up and was like, "A homie I need you to do me a favor?"

I'm looking him up and down like what the hell you talking about, so I respond with an attitude, "Who the hell are you!" Like I said earlier everyone wants a hook up, so can you guess what the next words were that came out of his mouth? "I need you to hook me up", and this is only one example, but it was happening to me just about all the time. So I decided to lay low for a couple of weeks until all the madness dies down. Juliet was surprised because during this time we spent a lot of needed time together according to her, but to me it was unwanted. Cheese and Perm was running things while I lay low. It was mainly Cheese, but Perm kept up with the weed at the grow house. Cheese did my part when it came to distributing and collecting, and he was a trust worthy and loyal soldier because he brought my money to me every night. I just couldn't believe how things were turning out, I mean, the money was good, everywhere we went we always got mad respect, there was no more waiting in line for anything especially at the clubs, but we did have a few big problems. First, there were haters, and secondly the police.

My first day back and later that night Cheese and I were riding to go make a sale on the west side of town, suddenly out of nowhere; red and blue lights starts flashing behind us, they gave us a few of those police burps, and then said over there mega phone, "Pull over!" See, I did make up one rule sense hearing about my home boy getting busted a few years ago, and that was no smoking weed while driving. Because if a cop walks up to your car and smells weed that's an automatic reason to search the car, and we have nine pounds in the trunk right now.

I pull over with both hands on the steering wheel, and then the cop says with his redneck southern accent, "How you boys doing tonight?"

"I'm fine sir and you"?

Not replying to my question he says, "I'm a need you boys to step out the car?"

"Sir, I don't mean any disrespect and I hope you don't mind me asking, but what did we do"?

"Look here, if you didn't notice the first time I didn't answer your question, so I'm not going to start now, now you two get your black asses out the car!"!

Next thing I know three more police cars pull up, and when we both saw that we looked at one another and I mumble under my breath, "Oh shit!"

So we both got out the car, and when we did, they immediately grabbed us and shoved us up against the rear doors of the car.

"Sir what did we do, what did we do"!

"Shut up", both cops shout! The one on me turns me around, takes a step back, and just stares at me for what seemed like for ever and then says, "Where do you work son, and don't you lie to me I'll take you in for false impersonation?"

So I didn't say anything, and I guess that pissed him off because he jacked me up by my collar, cut off my breath, and said, "You think you bad boy, hell you not shit to me, I know you're a drug dealer, and when I prove it your ass will be going away for a very long time!" I think he could see that I couldn't breathe; he cracked a crook smile, let me go, and then replied, "You boys have a good night."

Why in the world did I title this section "Mad Respect", because there's nothing about respect when it comes to crooked shit like this?

CHAPTER 13
MOVING UP

The Hook up

Times are definitely changing in the weed business, and when I say this I mean big time, and especially for us. The money we had been making before was now being cut in half and it seemed to happen over night. First, hydro-weed was on the scene and was taking over; though it gave smokers a better high it was also higher in price and less in quantity, none the less, it had become very popular and hustlers where buying it up. Secondly, dealers had started dipping there weed in embalming fluid, and yes you heard me right they were dipping there weed in the same stuff that was being put in dead people, can you believe that? If you asked smokers about why they liked smoking this stuff so much they would tell you it's because it's high was twenty times more powerful then regular weed. Last of all, these heavy smokers started smoking a more powerful drug, and that drug was crack cocaine. I always had my doubts about this drug and really didn't want to fool with it, but it just boomed on the scene and became a real money making drug, and you know me I'm all about making money. So one day I called Perm and Cheese and told them that I needed to talk to them. I drove and picked them up and we went to the Waffle House.

"Look yaw, we have to do something!"

"What's wrong Dre", Perm asked?

"What you mean, we haven't been making much of anything when it comes to money, and you going to ask me what's wrong!"

"That's not my fault so you don't need to come at me like that"!

"Let me tell you something homie, you don't do shit but ride and I can do this shit without you"!

"Homie Fuck you"!

"Naw homie fuck you"!

"What you want to do then Dre"!

"Shit it don't matter to me"!

We both stand up to go outside to handle this, when Cheese says, "Both of yaw calm the fuck down, yaw making a scene"!

He gets up and grabs Perm by the arm and shovels him back in his seat, and then he says to me, "Come on Dre", pointing to my seat, so I hesitantly sit down.

"Dre, I don't mean know disrespect, but you right we do need to find something new", turning and facing Big Perm, he says, "Perm, Dre and I rode around all night last night and we only made $900.00".

"You mean to tell me yaw only made $900.00 all of last night"?

"Yeah"

After I calmed down I was like, "Look, my bad Perm I didn't mean to come at you like that", so we gave one another some dap and he let it go, "But this hasn't been just this night it's been going on for a while now".

"So what you wanting to do homie", Perm asks?

"Shoot I don't know, all I know is that I have pounds and pounds of weed I need to get off".

There was a silence for about a minute, and then Cheese says, "I have a plan, you might not like it, but I think we could make three times the money a day that we are making now".

Perm and I look at one another and I kind of had an idea of what he was talking about, and then I say, "Selling crack".

"I'm telling you Dre there's a lot of money to be made".

"Ok Cheese, it seems like you have a plan, so lay it on me".

"I have a homie who buys weed from us who sells weight in powder; I can go to him and see how all this crack stuff works".

"What you mean how all this crack stuff works", Perm asks?

"Well you know you have to cook the powder up some how, and then you do something else to it to make it get hard and turn into crack".

"So what's your plan Cheese", I asked?

"I'm a go buy a certain amount from him and have him show me what I need to do, and then while we ride around selling weed I'm a sell the crack at the same time and see how things go, and then we can go from there".

Cheese plan wasn't that bad of an idea, so we decided to try it, and after he built up some clientele it was on. Needless to say he sold out in one night and made $1500.00, and that's all I needed to see, I wanted in on this part of the game.

Cheese introduced me to one of his girlfriends' cousin who was from South Carolina who they called "motor city", why I have no earthly idea. I didn't want any two bit weight, I wanted big time weight so he told Cheese to have us come down to South Carolina, and when the time was right we did. When I say this dude had some dope, I mean he had a whole lot of dope. I told him what I wanted to do, how much I wanted to spend, and how often I would be coming down to see him. He was down, so I put the plan into motion. I spent $50,000.00 for ten birds or kilos. In each kilo there is 36 ounces, so total I had a total of 360 ounces of pure cocaine, at a $1000 an ounce; now you do the math. We traveled back to Knoxville nervous as hell, when we got back we went straight to the grow house that we had and went to work on making this cocaine crack. Now we just had to find a way of getting our dope out there in the neighborhoods in the midst of other dope dealers, and I had the perfect person in mind; Robert. I know yaw remember the guy I spoke to in the beginning of the book?

THE DRIVE TO SOUTH CAROLINA; AND

T-BONE COMES ABORD

Before we go any further let me explain how we transported the dope back and forth, because this was a brilliant plan: First, we went to the junk yard and found and old beat up truck that was shaped like a UPS truck. Second, I found and racist red-neck who all he wanted was beer, cigarettes, $500.00, and a quarter ounce of crack to strip down and fix up that old truck. Third, once he fixed it up we took it to my homie on the east-side of town were I had him paint and polish it a dark brown; the same color as a UPS truck. One day while a UPS worker was parked making a delivery Cheese went up to it and started taking pictures of it on all sides. Fourth, we found a nerdy looking black guy who took these pictures and helped us make our truck look just like a real UPS truck, but we used reusable stickers on the truck and on the tags so we could change the truck when need be. I'm telling you we had or at least we thought we had a brilliant plan and set-up. Last of all, we hired two guys who we paid very well who would drive to South Carolina, park the truck where Motor City told us to, the next day several UPS boxes would be on what was once and empty truck, they would change and put on there brown uniforms, put the stickers and fake tag back on the truck, and head back to Knoxville. Once in Knoxville they would pull to the back of the grow house I had where someone would be waiting on them and then they would take off and do the same thing every 4 months for us. Now you tell me was this an awesome plan or what? I told you, and it all came from yours truly.

Like I said in the previous section I knew who I could get to help us get this dope off, so I go riding to the northwest side of town looking for him. I use to seeing him on the block from time to time, but lately I haven't seen him at all. I rode around the block a couple times not seeing him, but seeing his homie T-bone. So Cheese and I pull over and gets out the car walking towards were T-bone is standing.

After giving T-bone some dap I ask, "A homie you know where Rob might be"?

"Naw, I haven't seen him in a couple days".

"Damn I was really, really hoping to talk to him".

"Well if I see him I'll let him know that you're looking for him".

"All right homie", I replied, I give him some dap and started walking off.

"A", he shouts when I get half way to the car, "Is it something I can help you with!"

Thinking to myself I don't even know this dude like this, but he does hang around with Rob maybe he could help.

"Let me talk to you in the car".

Cheese starts shaking his head no, and then says, "I don't trust this man Dre."

"Let me handle this homie, everything is going to be all right trust me".

We get in the car and I break down what we were planning to do and why I was looking for Rob. I didn't tell T-bone everything just enough to get his interest. T-bone was down with helping us and he didn't disappoint. As soon as he came aboard the money started pouring in. He actually set up some of our bigger deals and helped up build top notch clientele, and before we knew it we were sitting around counting at my grow house almost $200,000.00, and we still had over 300 ounces of dope left; to this success I credit T-bone, and that's why I don't care what Perm or Cheese says he's part of this crew now, like it or not.

BALLING OUT OF CONTROL

One day we were all over Big Perms house playing Madden, dominoes, watching music videos, and smoking weed.

"Milton, you see this", T-bone shouts!

Coming out the kitchen I'm like, "What's up T"?

"The NBA All-Star game is coming to Atlanta".

"And"!

"What the hell you mean "and", I think we should make plans to go".

Shaking my head I start thinking to myself, this brother has lost his damn mind, then Perm chimes in, "You know what Dre, that's not a bad idea".

T-bones comes in the kitchen where we were and sat down at the kitchen table and started rolling up a blunt.

"Perm, toss me one of those brew's out the fridge", I ask? He grabbed him one and literally tossed me one and then came and sat down at the table with us.

"When is the All-Star game", Perm asks?

"I know it's this month sometime".

"I think it's like mid-February", T-bone through in.

"Well, find out what day it's on so we can make plans to go".

"I think it's like a whole weekend event; I know the dunk contest and the three point contest is something I would want to see". So we ended that conversation on that note, and two days later T-bone called my cell with the information that we needed.

"Hello"?

"What's up Milton, this T-bone"!

"Man, I know who you are, what's up"?

"I looked up the All-Star game on the internet and found out that it starts on the 10th."

"Damn that's right around the corner"

"I know, do you think we'll make it"?

"Oh hell yeah homie it's definitely going down".

"Yes"!

"So make sure you bring your girl because we going down here to floss and show off".

"I'm down with that".

"Come on over so you can celebrate with us".

"What we celebrating"?

"Homie we going to an All-Star", and then we hung up!

Cheese was the first one here and sometimes I get the feeling that he's a little jealous of T-bone. I say this because every time I say T came up with an idea, he always says, "I don't like him Milton."

When everyone arrived I told my plans, and I had big ones to. My plan was to floss like I never had before. Everyone had a woman except T-Bone; and honestly, he wasn't the best looking dude, so in my eye's he was just shit out of luck. I had Juliet call and book us three rooms at the Hyatt Regency. See, this wasn't just our time to shine as a click it was also time to put our women on display and let them do what they do. That week Juliet and I hit the malls and shopped like we never had before buying nothing but the best. I spent over $20,000 on clothes, shoes, and jewelry for me and my baby. Two days before our trip to Atlanta I rented three black Cadillac Escalades from Avis and that was on a Tuesday, and the next day we headed out traveling in comfort and style.

When we arrived in the ATL it was on. The Hyatt Regency treated us as if we were super-stars, I mean, there was valet parking, bell hoppers, Jacuzzi's in the room, and room service that made and had anything you wanted. Juliet and I did a little sight seeing and spent a little quality time together, but when the sun went down it was the click's time to kick it. We hit every night club and strip club we possibly could. We met famous rappers, actors, and ball players both basketball and football. A couple of them we even sat down and got messed up with. By the end of our first night we were so messed up we had to get the girls to come pick us up, and I could tell that Juliet was pissed off.

The tickets I bought weren't exactly floor side seats, but they were pretty damn close, I mean, we were right up on the action. We saw the three point shoot-out live, the dunk contest live, and most importantly we saw the All-Star game live and it was off the chain to; we even met a few of the ball players after the game. But you know I saved the best part of the trip for last; and that's the fine ass black women that are in Atlanta. My second night there the fellows and I hooked up with a few of the strippers from the strip club. The only one that wasn't with us was T-Bone because he claimed he wasn't in the mood, so that was his lost. These girls took us to there place and they gave us each a private strip show of our own if you know what I mean. Damn I had a good ass time in Atlanta, and the sad thing was when time came for us to leave, I really wasn't ready, but I already knew we had to.

"Dre you ready to go", Perm asked as we were loading our luggage in the SUV?

"Hell naw".

"Me either".

"Shoot I just might move down here", T-Bone replies out of nowhere.

As soon as he said that Perm, Cheese, and I looked at one another and busted out laughing; looking confused T-Bone replied, "What's so damn funny"?

As he was getting in the car Cheese says, "It's like Ice Cube said homie, it's a nice place to visit, but I wouldn't want to live here".

CHAPTER 14
BUSTED

THE SMOOTH SET-UP

Recently I've been feeling the need to try and make things right between me and Juliet, but for some reasons all my attempts have failed. These last few months have been very frustrating for me, and that's why I'm over Perms house so I can get some stuff off my chest, my heart, and my mind.

"Man I don't know what else to do", I reply as I blow out the weed smoke I just inhaled.

He takes the blunt from me he responds, "So why do you think she's tripping so much now?"

"Hell I don't know, maybe some of her so called home girls calls themselves telling on me again".

"Dre I don't know, maybe she just fed up with the bullshit".

"What the hell you mean "the bullshit", shit I take good care of her, I make sure she stay clean and I make sure she stay satisfied in the bedroom".

"Dre, I'm your boy and I have to keep it real with you, you might get mad, but we, and I said "we" not just you, we be doing some messed up stuff on these girls and you know it".

After he said all he had to say he got me to thinking, and when you smoking weed thinking is the last thing you want to be doing. Because even though he was right in my mind he was wrong and I must be honest, he almost lost a friend that day.

I think he could feel that I was a little upset and frustrated, so he says to me, "Dre you know we like brothers and I wouldn't want to lose you as a brother over no bullshit, but the way you was doing Juliet, I also did to Denise, I'm not telling you something I've heard I'm telling you something I've experienced, so my advice is this; tell her how you feel before it's too late."

"You know why I'm so pissed off Perm"?

"Why"?

"Man, I paid for a four day get away to a chalet in the mountains, and you know what she told me; she told me that she would rather go to Atlanta with her friends then spend some time with me".

"Damn Dre that's messed up".

Just then my cell phone rings; its T-bone and I haven't heard from this cat in about two months and I was starting to get worried. The last time I talked to him he was suppose to be going to visit some family out of town. I gave him nine ounces so he could go and set up some new connections, but for some reason he didn't keep in contact with me.

"Man where the hell have you been"!

"Chilling with my family I told you that".

"Yea but business before pleasure"

"My bad homie"

"Why are you just now calling me then"!

"I just got caught up with the family Milton you know how it is".

"So what's up on the money tip is everything good"?

"Everything good homie, they loving it up here, and yes I do have your money if that's what you trying to get to".

"If I wanted to know about my money I know how to ask about it"!

"I'm just saying homie I got you".

"Are you in town yet"?

"Not yet but I'm on my way; how is everything on the home front".

"Shoot everything gravy, business is always on the up".

"Oh yeah, my homie up in Elizabethan wanted us to come up that way for a drop off".

"What's the price"?

"Ten g's and he said he needs it bad".

"How far away are you"?

"About three hours".

"Is he going to be at the same spot"?

"Yeah"!

"Well tell him I'm on my way", and then we hung up.

I drove by myself even though Perm and Cheese didn't want me to, but I was in one of those moods were I just wanted to be alone. I've done business with homie before whose name is Chris, so I knew it was going to be cool and an easy transaction. Last time I was up there Chris had some fine ass freaks, and I figured since I had the chalet all ready paid for I'll just get one of those freaks up there and take her. As I was driving a really bad rain storm hit and I had to pull over several times until it calmed down. It just seemed as if something was trying to tell me not to go, but I was just so damn determined. Before I left I rolled up three big blunts of that dro weed, so you know I was smoking good the whole trip. When I got there I pulled over at the gas station and I rolled up one more blunt because I wanted to pull up looking like I'm the shit. I fire the blunt up and pull out the gas store parking lot. I turn the music up in my car bumping Paul Wall's "Sitting Side Ways", you couldn't tell me anything as I was driving towards homies apartment. Leaning back in my seat, with one hand on the steering wheel and a blunt in the other, I pulled into his drive way and as soon as I got ready to turn the stereo down I looked up and blue and red lights were everywhere. As soon as I turned my head to see what was going on there was and ATF agent in all black with a sawed off shotgun pointed to my head, and he said 16 words I'll never forget, "Leave your hands where I can see them or I'll blow your got damn head off!"

They came and snatched me out the car and slammed me to the ground. They hand cuffed me, lifted me up and had me watch as they popped my trunk. They pulled up the spare tire, and then pulled out the ten ounces of dope that I had in it. They patted me down and took the $4800 that I had in my pocket, and then took me over and sat me in the police cruiser. But I notice something; they didn't have a police dog present, so how did they know exactly where to go to find the dope. After what seemed like hours of sitting in the back of the cruiser one of the agents finally came over and spoke to me. Out of all the stuff this agent said and threaten me with; it would be only four words that I heard him say, "T GAVE YOU UP".

T-BONE MOVES IN AND TAKES OVER

There was only three other people besides myself that knew how I transported my dope from South Carolina; Perm, Cheese, and T. I usually picked up the drop offs by myself, but every now and then one of them would be with me and most the time it was T. That's why I think the two drivers that I had felt comfortable enough with leaving the dope with T. T knew that Perm and Cheese didn't know what was going on and his plan worked to perfection. He messed up and destroyed my operation and started making plans to start his own. After about two or three hours everyone started looking for me, and Cheese called T to see what was going on.

"Hello".

"What's up homie this is Cheese".

"What's going on homie"?

"Man I'm not trying to get you worried, but have you heard from Milton"?

"I talked to him earlier and he said he was going to handle some business up in Johnson City, why is everything ok"?

"Shit I guess, damn it's not like him not to answer his phone".

"You know how he is when it comes to those freaks".

"Yeah you right, I just hope he's all right, if you hear from him tell him to call me"?

"I got you, as soon as I hear from him I'll call you, better yet, I'll tell him to call you".

"All right homie I talk to you later".

You want to know what's sad about this whole situation. The way T-bone described me to Cheese is exactly how I am. I can't believe that this brother did me like this. Cheese was right about him the whole time, but now it's too late. In my mind I can see this low down dirty brother laughing at me, and telling all his homies, "That I was a sucker", but he's right. I thought he was my friend, I thought he was my homie; I thought he was my brother, but now I see that I was wrong.

So to keep a long story short T eventually did take over. As long as the transporters kept getting paid they didn't care who they was dropping off to. He even threatens Perm and Cheese to the point that they left the game alone and started laying low. But stay tuned because I have an even bigger surprise to come.

CHAPTER 15
DOING TIME AGAIN

THE PHONE CALL HOME

"**M**ilton, the TBI needs a huge favor from you", the agent states with a serious look on his face.

"What you mean you need a favor from me"!

"Look Milton, Tyshaun did what we asked him to do and by doing that he made things a whole lot easier for himself."

I know he isn't asking me to do what I think he is, that's what I'm thinking to myself, then I reply, "What you mean?"

"We told him to bring us someone that's pushing, and he brought us you, now we asking that you do the same thing."

I must be honest, the thought did cross my mind, but if I did that that would make me a low down dirty ass snitch like T, so I reply, "The hell with that, I'm not no damn snitch!"

The agent jumped up, slammed his palm on the table making it sound like a bomb with off, and then lean over the table and replied, "Son you don't know what your doing, you're not using your head, I could get you two years probation or I can see to it that you go up the river!"

"I'm not a damn snitch", on the outside I look cool, but on the inside I'm scared as hell.

He motion to the guard to come and get me and as the guard was taking me out he stopped us and said to me, "Trust me, you about to pay for that decision boy and that's a promise", and he wasn't lying either; that's one promise that he kept.

After they booked me, they gave me a sleeping mat and a raggedy looking blanket and then lead me up to my cell block. These cell blocks were just like the ones in the Alaskan jail, but far worst. When the guards open the door one of them shoved me in and then said, "Good luck."

Looking back at him I think to myself what the hell is he talking about? As soon as I walked in, I saw what he was talking about. Their was nothing but big red neck white boys, and when they saw me it got so quite you could hear a pin drop. I started hearing knuckles cracking and then the ones sitting at the table all stood up in unison. They looked like they were ready to attack, I could see the anger in their eye's, and feel the hatred in their hearts, so I started bracing myself for what was coming next. Just then one of them walked out of the first cell and replied, "We got us another nigger ass to beat."

I already knew what was coming next, so I thought to myself I don't have much of a choice. I put my head down and drew back with all my might and surprised punched the one that made that comment, and that would be the only punch I would through. All those white boys rushed me and they started beating my ass like never before. Kicking and stomping me in my head and ribs; I thought they were going to kill me, but just then the guards came in and pulled me out. They basically started dragging me to another cell block and as they were pulling me along I tried to resist because honestly I was scared as hell, but resisting didn't work and they threw me into a new cell block. Bracing my self for what was to come, with my blurred vision, and squinting out my half swollen eyes; I noticed that in this cell block there were black dudes and they were actually trying to help me. That kind of put my heart at ease, but honestly, I was still a little jumpy and shook up.

The jail was severely over crowded and there where mats lined up all along the floor against the wall. The stench in the cell block was very bad and you could see the mold growing in the corners of the walls. The windows were covered with metal slabs and no sunlight was able to get into the block.

As I lay on my mat for the next couple of hours nursing my swollen eye and sore and bruised body; I notice a pay phone on the wall and decide I better call Juliet since they didn't give me my free phone call. The operator asked me my name and I give it, but to my surprise a very familiar male voice answers on the other end of the phone.

"You have an inmate call from the Carter County Jail from: Milton; will you accept the charges?"

"Yeah"

With anger in my voice I say, "What the hell you doing answering my phone bitch!"

"Man what the hell do you want?"

"Put Juliet on the phone you damn snitch!"

Slamming the phone down, he shouts, "Juliet, telephone!"

"Who is it?"

As he passes the phone, he says, "Your punk ass ex-boyfriend!"

"Hello?"

"Oh, so now I'm your punk ass ex-boyfriend!"

"What do you want Milton?"

"What you mean what I want, don't you know that T set me up and I'm locked up right now because of him!"

"No Milton don't blame him, you locked up because of you."

"How the hell am I locked up because of me, the TBI agents told me what the deal was!"

"He only did what he had to do; hell, your low down sorry ass was so damn cheap you didn't want to pay nobody any money."

"Juliet, what the hell are you talking about, I took care of everyone that rolled with me and you know that, you know what; I'm starting to think that you where in on this with him!"

"Look I have to go, we're moving and my man is waiting on me; and by the way you won't be seeing your son."

"What the hell are you talking about I'm his daddy"!

"No, he has a new daddy, and his name is Tyshaun."

"You know what fuck you bitch, I hope you get everything you deserve", and then she hung up the phone in my face! I have to be honest; I broke down and started crying. Out of my anger I started slamming the phone receiver against the phone base a few times. I had to gather myself and get my mind right and try to understand what had just taken place. Later that day a guard came and gave me a number I could use to make my one phone call with and it was only good for one use, so I called my dad and told him everything that had happen. I told him about being set up by T and how T and Juliet are now together. I told him how she did me on the phone when I called her. I also told him that I wanted to see him at my court date tomorrow; and he promised me that he would be there. As I lay here on my mat I start thinking how everything is starting to fall a part; maybe this is it for me, maybe this is how my life is suppose to end. I just can't help but think about when Juliet and I first met, I wouldn't have ever guessed that we would end up this way, but I also didn't see myself being locked up in Carter County either. So go figure.

STANDING BEFORE THE JUDGE (UNFAIR JUDGEMENT)

"ALL RISE", CRIMINAL COURT IS NOW IN SESSION, THE HONORABLE ROBERT J. COOK IS PRESIDING, PLEASE TURN OFF ALL CELLPHONES AND NO TALKING WHILE THE JUDGE IS TALKING", the bailiff shouts with his booming commanding voice!

THE PATHS THAT LIE AHEAD

The judge comes in and takes his seat behind the podium, and then the bailiff shouts, "YOU MAY ALL BE SEATED", and we take our seats! Looking out in the audience I see my dad and Big Perm sitting right up front, and that really did my heart some good.

There were eight people that went up before the judge before me; two were people from the audience, and six were inmates sitting were I was; and all inmates were placed over on an isolated side of the courtroom away from everyone else. As each one of these individual went up before the judge I started noticing a pattern taking place. I noticed that whenever a black or Hispanic stood before the judge he was rude and mean as hell, and the penalties for us were a whole lot stiffer then on the whites. Allow me to give an example: Whenever the whites went up, the judge was more understanding and let certain offenses go. One white guy had been before this judge six times in a two year period, and the most he ever got was probation. While one of the black guys sitting over with us, and this was his first time before the judge mind you; got a five year prison sentence for basically the same offense the white guy had. To me this was very unfair and I knew this wasn't going to be a good thing for me.

When it was my turn to stand before the judge he looked at me as if I disgust him and he took a long pause before he even said anything.

The DA stands up and says, "Your honor Mr. Lusser was arrested last night with over nine ounces of cocaine and three ounces of crack, and the people are looking to charge him with drug trafficking because he crossed multiply county line with these drugs in his trunk."

The judge writes something down and then looks up says, "Now what do you have to say for yourself young man"? Hell, I didn't know what to say so I just shrugged my shoulders.

"See that's the problem with you drug dealers you all don't have any common sense and you all don't have any class, I hope you have had some home training?"

"Yes sir".

"Well I'm a set Mr. Lusser's bond at $1000".

"Your honor Mr. Lusser isn't from this area and we feel that he is a high flight risk, so the court is asking that you set his bond a little higher then that?"

"Where are you from son?"

"Knoxville."

"How did you get all the way up here"? Again, I just shrug my shoulders.

"It seems that that's all you know how to do, so at the DA's request I'm a set bond at $500,000 *(My heart dropped in my chest),* and we will reset this court hearing three months from now where we will appoint Mr. Lusser a lawyer, son you may take your seat", and that's how my first appearance before the judge went.

Did I have the money to make my bond? I sure did but the money was back at home. I waited a couple of hour before calling, and after further talks with my dad I decide to wait on posting bond. I mean, I know I can do three months, and we both anticipated that I would be getting out then, but boy would we be in for a big surprise.

CHAPTER 16
A NEW MISSION

WRITING LYRICS WHILE LOCKED UP

Like I said in the previous chapter getting out wasn't going to be as easy as I thought, and allow me to share the reason why. About a month before my court date a fight broke out in my cell block; now I must be honest, I did have a hand in it, but I didn't start it. When the guards came in and broke it up they took each inmate involved to the hole. They question us one inmate at a time, and I held my ground; meaning I didn't snitch. The next day I found out that someone told the investigating guard that I started the fight, and it all went down hill from there. I miss my court date and it was reschedule six months out, the judge revoked my bond, I wasn't allowed any phone calls or commissary, and to top it all I had to spend the next (60) days in the hole. The first few days all I did was cry out of frustration; how can someone be on top of the world one minute and the next be at their lowest? The shit just wasn't making sense to me and as I lay here on this hard ass mat thinking looking back over my life I began to realize something. I always blamed others for my problems: I blamed my mama, my daddy, my brother, my baby mamas, and even the system; but for some reason I never blamed myself or took responsibility for my own decision making and actions. I had an old King James Bible that one of the inmates getting out gave me and I started reading from the book of Genesis and didn't stop until I finished Revelation. It took me four days to do it, and I did it about five times while I was in here. After the fifth time I decided to put my feelings on paper; at first it started out as just writings, but they eventually turned into rhymes. These rhymes expressed how I felt at the time and a lot of them were directed at that snitch ass brother T-bone.

When I finally got out the hole the whole cell block had changed; there were only a few faces that I recognized and that recognized me. I stayed strictly to myself this time writing my rhymes and reading my bible. As time went on some of the inmates started working out doing push-ups and sit-ups; they even had a water bag that they would use to do arm curls with. I was starting to get bored so I decided to join them, hell I wasn't doing nothing but laying down all the time anyways. One day I was lying down tired after a good workout and was getting ready to dose off when all of a sudden I heard someone in the dayroom making beats on the table and someone rhyming to it. The beat was tight and the brother flowing was all right, so I decided to go to the dayroom and join in on the flow session bringing some of the stuff that I had been working on, and they loved it.

"Damn I didn't know you could flow", the one making the beats replied?

"Me either homie that was tight as hell", the one flowing added.

"Shoot homie the beat you was making set it off, what are you a producer or something"?

"Something likes that, I have a studio, but none of these brothers up here are serious about anything".

"I have a homie back home who has a full professional studio, and he be making those tight ass beats".

"Where you from"?

"Knoxville".

Putting his hand out to give me some dap he says, "I'm Squirt".

His home boy follows, "I'm Dub"

Giving them both some dap I respond, "Dre", and it was own from that moment on. All we did was make music; we even put on a few mini shows in the dayroom. I mean, he would make the beats on the table and we would rhyme to it.

From time to time I would call Big Perm and let him hear what was going on. We would make beats and flow in the background over the phone so he could hear us, and then I would listen to the beats he had made or had just started working on.

"It sounds like you ready Dre".

"Why you say that"?

"Because back in the day I couldn't get you to write raps for nothing, but now that you are; you putting it down".

"So what's next"?

"Don't worry about that little homie, you just keep writing, and when the right time come I'll have everything ready", and we hung up.

BEING RELEAED WITH A NEW MISSION IN MIND

Now that I've been locked up for almost two years now, my mind set is starting to change. For example: I made up my mind that I was definitely out the dope game; honestly, I just couldn't take being locked up like a caged animal and being told what to do all the time. Seeing nothing but these four mold invested, dirty walls for the last two years made my emotional state fluctuate up and down and I was quietly very unstable. There were days when I felt like giving up and wanted to kill myself; but then there were days where I did nothing but think about my kids and all the things that I've missed, and was determined to make it out. This mental struggle started to become a challenge, and the only way I could deal with it was writing; so that's what I did. I had note book after note book of writings where I expressed my pain, and you can see the days when I was up and the days when I was down. I 100% blamed T-bone for what has taken place in my life these past two years and I definitely plan to revenge what he has done to me, but my revenge isn't going to be with guns and violence; my revenge is going to be with my mind and mouth, I plan to blow this cat plum the fuck out the water with my words. I have a court date coming up very soon and I'm so damn nervous. I've been hoping and praying so bad that this judge sets me free so I can start my life where I left off. My life has been in the "to be continue" mode for two years and now it's time for the next chapter to begin.

"Lusser let's go you have court this morning", the guard shouts!

He didn't have to call me twice I jumped up and was at the door in a second flat, "Yes sir I'm ready." He shackles both my wrists and my ankles together and leads me to the elevator. The whole time I'm walking to the court room all I'm thinking about is the Sun Sphere. See, the Sun Sphere is a big gold globe in the sky, held up by multiple blue huge steel beams, and has an elevator that takes you up and down. They say it uses to be a restaurant where people could go and eat, honestly I don't know about that, but the one thing I do know is that this is what makes Knoxville the great city that it is. It's a sight like no other; it's been up since the 1982 World's Fair and is a major land mark, well, at least in my opinion it is.

As I sit waiting for my time to stand before the judge I see my dad come in, and right behind him was the lawyer that he got me from Knoxville that I heard was really good. I had a court appointed lawyer three months ago, but that dude was sorry as hell; he's the reason I'm still in here right now. Wanting me to take a deal that would put me worst off then what I already am, the hell with that. My dad through me the thumbs up sign and as soon as I seen that I knew I was getting out today.

My lawyer comes over to me and says, "I need to speak with you in the back room", so I get up and follow him.

"So the plan today is to have you released."

"Hell yeah"!

"But there's a catch, the DA is asking for a ten year sentence, all of which can be served on probation, and that's what I'm going to be asking for today if that's alright with you."

113

Shoot all I'm thinking about is getting out of here so I'm like, "That's cool as long as I can get out today."

"If you accept this deal, which honestly isn't much of a deal, you will definitely be going home."

"But why you say this isn't a deal?"

"Well, what the judge wants to do is send you to prison for twelve years, and I didn't like that judgment for a first time offender, so what I talked them into doing was giving you ten years probation counting the time you've done so far towards that, which means you'll actually do eight years probation instead of ten, your dad said how bad you wanted out and I did what I could to get you out."

"I understand; if this is the best you could do shit lets do it then."

We walk back out in the courtroom and I take my seat back were the inmates sit; about thirty minutes later the bailiff calls me up and my lawyer and I went up to the podium, and the judge really let me have it.

"You know what Mr. Lusser I think the state is making a very big mistake with you today, putting you back on the streets isn't going to help anyone its only going to waste more taxpayers money, in my opinion once a drug dealer always a drug dealer, there's something in my heart that's telling me to send you on up the road, but the DA and your lawyer have agreed on a deal, which you have accepted right?"

"Yes your Honor."

"You know what son I'm only giving you one chance, the next time you come before me and you will be back, it's to prison with you do you hear me?"

"I won't be back"

"Oh yes you will I guarantee it." In defense of my lawyer he didn't give him a chance to say anything.

The judge takes a deep breath and then sighs, "Mr. Lusser will be placed on ten years probation, the time that he has done here will count against his probation so he will serve an eight year probation sentence plus court cost and fee's, he is to be released under his own supervision and must report to a state probation officer with in 15 days", and this would be the last time I would stand before this judge.

After that the guard took a few inmates back to their cell blocks and I was one of them. It usually takes them an hour or two to come get those who have been released, but not me; as soon as the guard opens the door he said, "Go get your stuff and come on", I was all smiles. I gave dap to all my homies and then I dipped out. I changed my clothes getting out that stripped green and white jumpsuit, and then they took me down the elevator; as soon as got off I saw my dad and we hugged one another like never before. I have to be honest I truly learned my lesson, and as we travelled back to Knoxville I couldn't sleep. I would pinch myself from time to time to make sure that I wasn't dreaming; all I wanted to see was the Sun Sphere and I finally did. I knew then I was home, and damn it felt so good to be home. I went by and seen everyone I was supposed to see: My mama, brother, Perm, Cheese, and especially my kids. I made some promises to them that to this very day I promise to keep. I also made some promises to myself and I didn't waste anytime getting started. If you never heard of me before; you damn sure about to know of me after all this shit goes down.

CHAPTER 17
A LEGAL HUSTLE

DOING IT THE RIGHT WAY

After my release I didn't waste anytime getting started. The very next day I was over at Perm's showing him the stuff that I had been working on while in jail. I shared with him my ideas and the direction that I wanted to take. He heard just about every song I had wrote, he seen the imagined that I wanted to portray, and he could also see the focus that I had in accomplishing this goal. See, I believed that if I took the success that I had in the dope game, and applied it to my music career I could be just as successful. Everyone knows how difficult it is to be a success in the music business and it's clear that only the hard working ones with the right people around them truly make it, and that's what I'm looking for.

The first song I started working on was entitled "Bet it All", and Perm gave me a hot ass track; this song had everyone in the studio moving and bouncing to the flow and the beat.

"Damn homie that's hot", Cheese shouts!

"Thanks homie", I replied, and then everyone started high fiving one another.

"Dre this song is hot, now all we have to do is add the hook and the adlibs, and we can add this one to the many more to come"!

"Perm I want to put together a five track album with five of my hottest songs and pass it out for free" you should've seen and heard the room after I said that. They got so quiet you could hear a pin drop and the looks where all looks of confusion.

"Man what the hell you mean free, this song is good enough for us to sell it, and trust me Dre people will buy it!"

"It's not that Perm, I want to build a buzz before I start selling, and if I build a successful buzz when time come people will run to buy." Normally it would be Perm with the bright idea, but this time it was me, and he couldn't argue with me because he knew I was right.

"Milton you sure that's what you want to do", Cheese ask?

"Yeah homie, just trust me, and I guarantee you we will make way more money then we ever did selling dope, but this time we going to do it the legal and right way."

Over the next three weeks I made the other five songs for this free album that I wanted to pass out, and trust me, all of them were club bangers. Here are the titles of the five songs in the order they are on the album: The first song was "Bet it All", the second song was "Regardless", the third song was "Can't be Stopped", the fourth song was "Snitches", and the fifth and final song was "A Too Real Solider"; where I featured Perm, Cheese, and my cousin Richard whose nickname was Richie. All these songs like I said were thumpers and trunk rattlers. Perm had 5000 cd made up with a cheap looking album cover of me, and we hit the streets passing them out. We passed out 2000 here in Knoxville at the night clubs, local grocery stores, and on the corners; we passed out a 1000 each in Nashville and Atlanta with the same strategy in mind, we ended our free album tour by passing out 500 in Chattanooga, and 500 in Greensboro; we went to Greensboro because that's were Perm was from.

As we were riding back from Greensboro, Perm looked over at me and asked, "Dre here we go; you sure you ready?"

I take a long slow deep breath and then replied, "As ready as I'm going to be."

Perm asked this question because he had some big plans for me as well, and little did I know that these are the plans that would shoot me into super stardom. Perm could see that I was dedicated to my new passion; outside of working and seeing my probation officer once a month, I was always in the studio working on something. My goal this time was to make my new album even better then my last one because this time it's going for $5 a piece. So as I'm leaned back in the passenger seat in Perm's car headed back home, I start to wonder to myself if I can pull it off, next I go to hoping I can pull this off, and finally I'm praying "PLEASE LORD HELP ME TO PULL THIS OFF!"

THE BUZZ IS BUILDING

It didn't take long at all for us to get what we were hoping for. Two days after being back from Greensboro Perm's house phone started ringing non-stop. It was ringing so much that he decided to let the answering machine pick it up, and people were leaving messages telling us how much they like the album, how tight the beats and flows are, and even asking when is the next one coming out. I think my homie is really regretting putting his number on the front of the album cover as a contact number.

One of the early results in my career of getting my name out there was that Perm booked me as an opening act for a platinum selling artist in Atlanta, and you know I put it down. Without a doubt I definitely had the crowd rocking and hyped up by the time he took the stage. They only paid me $800 for doing it, but I didn't care; all I wanted to do was get my name out there, and my plan was working. I received calls from all over to come and perform as an opening act. Some jobs paid, but not very much; the highest I made was that $800 I spoke of, but $25 was the least I was paid. Some jobs didn't pay at all money wise, but the experience that it gave was worth way more then money. The one thing that I loved to see was people dancing and grooving to the music that I made.

One day Perm, Cheese, and I were riding around sight seeing; that's what we called riding around doing nothing. I was driving my new but used

2004 ocean blue jeep Cherokee and I made a stop at a red light. Right then the most amazing thing in my life happens; the car right next to us was bumping my song "Regardless", and not only were they bumping it they were also singing it word for word. I looked over at Perm and Cheese in amazement, and we all started smiling.

"Damn fam, do you see and here this"?

"Hell yea, I'm telling you Dre it's our time", the light turns green and then we pulled off.

After seeing all that, I decided that I would go to the night club this weekend. Perm and Cheese had been trying to get me to go out for a while now, but for some reason I just wouldn't go. I hadn't been to a night club since my release and just the thought of it made me a little nervous. Don't ask me why because I couldn't tell you, but when the weekend came I made up my mind that I was going; and I'm truly glad that I did. When we got there and started walking in I'm seeing people that I hadn't seen in years, and as we walked through the crowd trying to find a table to sit at we was getting mad love and respect from everyone. I mean, the women was out in full force looking and smelling so damn good; I have to be honest and don't laugh, but I haven't had sex since I've been released, and right now I'm plotting on whose going home with me tonight. All of a sudden, "Bet It All" came on. Let me make sure that you heard me; my song "Bet It All" came on and it got the club jumping. Everyone flocked to the dance floor and it got packed quickly. Just then Perm and Cheese come running over all hyped up and jumping up and down shouting, "THIS MY HOMIES SONG", pointing at me at the same time!

Next thing I know as the song is playing the DJ comes on the speakers shouting, "This is a local artist by the name of Dreweed, and it has been brought to my attention that he's in the house tonight, so before you leave show the young man some love because he's definitely going to put Knoxville on the map!"

As people came over to give me some dap; it was right then when I realized that this is what I'm destine to do, or is it?

NEEDING SOME CASH; I GOT YOU HOMIE

Phone rings, "Hello?"

"What's up homie, what you up to", Cheese asks?

"Shoot chilling, just got off work."

"Have you finished that song you were working on?"

"I just finished writing my lyrics now all I have to do is go put them down."

"Oh ok, when the next time you heading to the studio?"

"Man probably later on tonight after I get me a little rest."

"I heard a couple of songs on the album, and I have to say; I'm very impressed with what you and Perm are doing."

"A man, I appreciate that, but don't forget about you homie."

"Me! Hell I didn't do anything!"

"Cheese trusts me, and I put this on everything; you're a very big part of what we doing."

The phone gets quiet for a second, and then he says, "Thanks homie that means a lot."

"I'll give you a call when I'm on my way to the studio."

"Ok"

"Peace out."

"Yep"

About thirty minutes after talking to Cheese as I'm relaxing watching some Sport center my cell phone rings again. This time it's Perm and he seems to be a little frustrated.

"What's up big homie; everything good", I ask as I answer the phone?

"Hell no, everything is just so damn fucked up!"

"What's wrong?"

"Man look, I don't have enough money to do what I wanted us to do."

"What did you want to do?"

"I wanted to purchase 20,000 cds; I wanted to build a website promoting our record company and your record; I wanted to have business cards printed up; I wanted us to get our business license; and I wanted us to be able to travel from city to city selling and promoting your record. Once I found out how much hotels and stuff would cost, I don't have near that much money to do anything I wanted to do!"

"Look homie don't even worry about it because I have everything under control."

"What you mean you have everything under control?"

"Perm trust me, I got it."

"Man what you mean, do you know how much money I'm talking about!"

"Perm, am I your homie?

"Yeah, but . . ."

"No! No buts, I said I got you then I got you. Do you trust me?"

"Yeah"

"I'm on my way", and then we hung up.

Before I went to the studio to finish the last song for my album, I called Perm and Cheese and had them meet me over at my dad's house. I don't know if yaw remember when I said in an earlier chapter about me putting up money and not letting anyone know what I was doing. Well, now yaw are about to find out where I was putting it. When we met up at my dad's, I told my dad that I needed to see the mattress in his room; because he switched out his for mine when I was locked up. I went to the kitchen and got a sharp butcher knife, and started cutting the edges of the mattress. A few minutes later I peeled back the shell of the mattress, and everyone's eye's in the room got big. They were standing there staring at one another in shock and breathless. The upper half of the mattress was stuff with nothing but 100's, 50's, and 20's wrapped up in several different zip lock bags. When I was stashing this money I never took the time to count what I was stashing, but after three and a half hours of counting the total amount was $750,124.00. We had more then enough to do what Perm wanted to do, and when we went to the studio to put the finishing touches on my album the mood was very high and up beat. We did what we had to do, so now it's on and there's no looking back.

CHAPTER 18
BLOWING UP

HITTING THE STREETS MAKING MONEY

N ow that my album is complete and all the art work has been done we now faced a whole new challenge; and that's how do we get the word out and get people to buy it. I know yaw are probably thinking that sounds easy, but trust me, it's a whole lot more complicated then you may think. Perm did exactly what he talked about doing in the previous chapter. He put together a website were we advertised my first free album (Which a person can order and still get for free), my new album (Which is going for five dollars), and the mission we are on (Which we are trying to change the game). He bought over 25,000 flyers and business cards for us to pass out as we promoted the album. During all this planning and for some reason we were constantly snapping at one another and the people who were trying to help us. Perm seemed stressed out and on the verge of being burnt out; Cheese was running around like a chicken with its head cut off, and all I was concerned about was getting these cds off. I mean, instead of buying 20,000 cds like we disgust, Perm decided on his own mine you to purchase 50,000. To me that was a bit too much, but he and Cheese really felt like we could get them off; so we booked hotel rooms all over the country from New York City to Los Angeles. The time we had set to hit the road was quickly approaching, and we knew a lot of hard work was going to be required in order to meet the expectations we had set for our selves; so here goes nothing.

When time came for us to hit the streets with my new album we hit them in a mad frenzy, and I have to say Perm's strategy really did work. We didn't care who you were if you were willing to buy we sold. I mean, we sold to Black, White, Hispanic, and Asian; we sold in front of big and small name grocery and clothing stores, we sold at four way stops, we sold not too far from music stores that had a lot of customer traffic, we sold in downtown areas, we sold at bus transits, and we even sold on the out skirts of these cities we traveled to housing projects. We flew and used rental cars on the whole trip we took. We started in New York City, next we went to Philly, next to Pittsburg, next to Detroit, next to Cleveland, next to Canton, next to Louisville, next to Charlotte, next to Columbia, SC, next to Miami, next to Atlanta, next to Jackson, MS, next to Dallas, next to San Antonio, next to Phoenix, next to Las Vegas, next to Sacramento, and last of all we finished up in Los Angeles. We sold out of cds in Dallas and Perm had to contact the cd company that we used to get 50,000 more reproduced and sent to us there, and by the end of our little mini tour we sold out of those to. Now we invested $80,000 in this whole trip and on my cds, but when it was all said and done, we made $500,000 in sales, so when we got back to Knoxville we were riding really high.

"Perm can you believe this shit", I asked!

"Dre I knew we were going to do good but I didn't think it would be like this"!

"So what's next on the agenda"?

"Man, just get you some rest because I have a feeling it's going to be a busy year for you".

After we got home and got settled this is what we decided to do with the money that was made on the trip: Since there were only three main people running things and putting all the hard work in and that was Perm, Cheese, and myself; we decided to put $200,000 up for company purposes and split the remaining $300,000 evenly amongst the three of us. I'm not trying to sound lame or anything, but that meant we each got "$100,000"! I had never made this much money outside of hustling and doing this made me believe in myself. I could tell that after all that negative stuff that took place in my life two years ago now a change for the better is coming, and it's only going to get better you just watch and see.

THE UNDERGROUND KING

"You're listening to Moss the Boss on 88.9 Knoxville's best in Hip-Hop and R&B. Last night on love it or hate it, we played a song by a local underground rapper by the name of Dreweed. Everyone must've loved it because every since I've came in the phones have been blowing up with request for this song. You wanted it and now you've got it, here's Dreweed with "The time has come", the DJ shouts over the radio early one morning.

My song comes on and Cheese is the only one up early enough to hear it, so he calls me, "Hello"?

"Milton, you need to put it on 88.9 right now"!

"Why what's up"?

"Just do it homie"! So I put it on 88.9 and it would forever change my life; I heard myself on the radio for the very first time.

"A yaw come in here", I shout at the same time turning the radio up! I was over at my girl-friends house so you know all of this caught me off guard. When I turned the volume up her and her sister got excited when they realized who it was; both started jumping, dancing, and shouting; then her daughter and son came running in and they started getting down to the beat to. All of this made me feel good and all I could do is just smile.

As I'm sitting at the kitchen table enjoying the moment; in my excitement I accidently hung up on Cheese. As soon as the song went off my cell phone rings again, and this time it's Big Perm.

"A homie I have some great news".

"You mean you have better news then me being on the radio"?

"Man, you're being played on the radio stations in Miami, Atlanta, Charlotte, and Dallas".

He was right that was great news, so I jumped up out my seat shocked but also excited, and asked, "How in the world do you know that"?

"Because my phone's been blowing up and people are telling me that we are".

"Damn homie that's fantastically great news"!

"Fantastically great; what the hell is that, but anyways I have something even better then that".

"Like what"?

"You need to have a seat for this one".

"I'm sitting"!

"The magazine "Underground Rappers" wants to do an interview with you".

"Yeah right; are you serious"!

"Yeah, they have crowned you the new underground king".

I had to take a minute because all of this is catching me off guard, then I asked, "When do they want me to do the interview"?

"They said in the next couple of months".

"Well I think we should shoot a video before then".

"Why you say that"?

"Because, imagine being played on the radio, having a video out, and then doing the interview".

With a little hesitation, he replies, "Yeah you right, but who can we get to shoot it"?

"Hell the university offers a video class, maybe we can find a student who is eager to show what they can do, and they might shoot it for little then nothing".

"I'm on it; I'll call you as soon as I find out what's up".

Two weeks after this conversation we found a young man who was down with helping us out. He was a white nerdy looking college student, so we had our doubts about his abilities at first, but once he heard the song and told us what he wanted to do; we knew then that we had our man. We had to purchase the cameras and monitors, but he did the editing and the final and finishing touches at his school. This video was superb, and when I say that, I mean that it was off the chain.

SELLING OUT THE CLUB

WOW!!! I really didn't see all this coming, and I bet none of yaw did either. After my interview with the Underground Rappers magazine I was crowned the underground king. My interview was both printed and televised on the music video station channel 21 and it quickly became a fan favorite. I became a very hot commodity and couldn't walk the streets by myself anymore. I mean, my music career started taking off and the buzz about my music wasn't the only thing people were talking about. I also made a little history in the process, and if you don't believe me check the Hip-Hop record books. The result of me promoting my album, doing that interview, and making that video helped me be the first unsigned artist to reach number one on the radio, and in music videos. This might sound good to some people, but trust me my life got very hectic.

Due to my success several things started taking place. First, there was a myth that I sold over a million underground records; which clearly wasn't true, but we let it ride. Then there was the talk of how we got the money to do what we did, and of course drugs were the main topic. Finally, calls were coming in from all over the country from night clubs wanting me to come and perform, so Perm and Cheese had me on a mission.

My cell rings, "Hello"?

"What's up Dreweed, all the kinks have been worked out and the club tour Perm told you about is ready", Cheese replied.

"So how many and how much"?

"Well according to Perm there's ten; Detroit, Canton, Cleveland, Louisville, Charlotte, Savannah, New Orleans, Miami, Atlanta, and finishing up right here in Knoxville".

"Damn that's a lot of cities"

"Yea, but guess how much you making per club"?

"Oh god how much"?

"$50,000"

"Yea right"!

"Milton I promise you, and all the money is up front".

"Cheese I'm with that, so when are we leaving out"?

"Tomorrow"

"Damn tomorrow"!

"Yea, but we'll be rolling out tonight".

I took a deep sigh and reluctantly replied, "I'm with it, and I'll be ready in about an hour".

"Naw don't rush, I'm pretty sure we have a little more time then that".

"Just call me when yaw ready".

"All right big homie"

"Peace" and we hung up.

About three hours later we were on the road, and as we rolled up to the first city on the club tour I was really caught off guard by what I saw. People were cheering chanting Dreweed. The women were yelling, and the guys were bumping my music reciting it.

I looked over at Perm and replied, "Damn homie is this shit for real"?

"You see it don't you; homie you done made it".

Looking over at him I say, "What you mean I done made it"?

"Homie look around; you have fans".

The last city we pulled up to was my home town and I was real nervous because this was home, and everyone wants to do good at home. I didn't know how people would receive me, but when we were pulling up it took us thirty minutes to get to the back door. As I'm sitting in the car getting my mind right Cheese taps on the window and gets in.

"A homie I have some great news".

"What's up"?

"The club is sold out".

Why he tell me that; now there's even more pressure on me to do well, and I was determined to do it.

Cheese cell rings he hangs up and asks, "You ready, because it's time"?

"I'm ready; go ahead I'll be right behind you".

He gets out and closes the door, I sit there for a few more minutes, and then I get out. He opens the backstage door, and I can hear the crowd cheering over and over again.

"Dreweed"!

"Dreweed"!

"Dreweed"!

As I make my way to the stage I gave dap to over 200 people; well, at least that's what it felt like. Perm hands me my mic we slap hands three times, I turn to Cheese and we slap hands three times, they turned to one another and they slap hands three times, and then we all three bumped mic's; we did this before each and every show. After that, the opening beat from my album comes on, and the butterflies really hit me hard. As Perm and Cheese pump the crowd up I stand behind the curtain with my head down thinking about what all it took to get here. I start moving my head to the beat getting my feel for the song as the curtain starts to rises. I lift up my head and the bright lights hit me right smack in my eyes, and then I exploded . . . .